THE LADY WITH THE PEN

The Lady with the Pen

Elise Wærenskjold in Texas

EDITED BY C. A. CLAUSEN
FOREWORD BY THEODORE C. BLEGEN

ARNO PRESS
A New York Times Company
New York • 1979

Editorial Supervision: Steven Bedney

Reprint Edition 1979 by Arno Press Inc.
Copyright 1961 by the Norwegian-American Historical Association
Reprinted by permission of the Norwegian-American Historical Association
Reprinted from a copy in the State Historical Society of Wisconsin Library

SCANDINAVIANS IN AMERICA
ISBN for complete set: 0-405-11628-4
See last pages of this volume for titles.

Manufactured in the United States of America

Library of Congress Cataloging in Publication Data

Waerenskjold, Elise Amalie Tvede, 1815-1895.
    The lady with the pen.

    (Scandinavians in America)
    Reprint of the ed. published by the Norwegian-
American Historical Association as v. 6 of its Travel
and description series.
    Includes index.
    1. Waerenskjold, Elise Amalie Tvede, 1815-1895.
2. Norwegian Americans--Texas--Kaufman Co.--Biography.
3. Frontier and pioneer life--Texas--Kaufman Co.
4. Kaufman Co., Tex.--Biography. I. Clausen, Clarence
Arthur, 1896-   II. Title. III. Series. IV. Series: Norwegian-American Historical Association.
Travel and description series ; v. 6.
[F392.K25W338 1979]   976.4'277'050924 [B] 78-15856
ISBN 0-405-11663-2

PUBLICATIONS OF THE
NORWEGIAN-AMERICAN HISTORICAL
ASSOCIATION
LIONEL G. THORSNESS, *President*

———

Board of Editors

THEODORE C. BLEGEN

C. A. CLAUSEN

EINAR HAUGEN

CARLTON C. QUALEY

KENNETH O. BJORK, *Managing Editor*

———

Travel and Description Series VOLUME VI

Elise Wærenskjold

The Lady with the Pen

Elise Wærenskjold in Texas

EDITED BY C. A. CLAUSEN
FOREWORD BY THEODORE C. BLEGEN

Norwegian-American Historical Association
Northfield, Minnesota
1961

Printed in the United States of America
at the North Central Publishing Company
St. Paul

Foreword

This book makes available in English the letters of a versatile "lady with the pen" who emigrated from Norway to Texas as early as 1847 and lived in the Lone Star State until her death in 1895. She won a measure of distinction by her championship of emigration from the Old World, her defense of Texas as a place for immigrant colonization, her unflagging devotion to writing, her deep convictions on the slavery issue, and her vibrant personality which left imprints on the Texan community of her choice.

Elise Amalie Wærenskjold was a devotee of the pen. She was not a professional writer, but all her life she wrote. Before she left Norway (at the age of thirty-two) she had published a small book and edited a magazine, and through her many years in America she penned letters and fugitive pieces, some of which appeared in newspapers or magazines. Her letters present a kaleidoscopic portrait of the immigrant colonies in Texas with which she cast her fortunes. They mirror people and everyday events as well as her own reflections, and they have historical interest as homely and simple chronicles of grass-roots immigrant experience. Yet, in themselves, they do not fully document or illustrate her importance. She was a cultural leader of piquant quality, a person of modern outlook, unintimidated by widely accepted conventions and in some ways ahead of her own times. Her pre-emigration record plus the force of her personality, as reflected in the lore of the community where she lived, helps to fill out the self-portrait disclosed in her letters.

She was known in Norway, before her emigration, as a woman of ideas and resolute courage. Reared in gentle circumstances, she had studied foreign languages, knew something about painting, and had a taste for books. As a girl of nineteen, in a time when women teachers were uncommon in Norway, she started and conducted an independent handicraft school for girls in the face of hostile criticism. In the 1840's she publicly advocated temperance, denounced drinking, and published a brochure aimed at nothing less than "eradicating drunkenness." This was a pioneering venture which, though it did not do away with the evil it combated, caused her to be hailed a century later as an early reformer. More in conflict with prevailing mores was her separation from a sea captain whom she had married in 1839—a friendly arrangement agreed upon in 1842. Divorces were rare in Norway and carried a social stigma. The event took on increased interest as time passed because Svend Foyn, the man she divorced, became the founder of Norway's whaling industry and a powerful and wealthy figure famous in Norwegian history. In later years Mrs. Wærenskjold made sparing reference to her first husband. The divorce, she said, was based on "incompatibility." Dr. Clausen, in his introduction to the letters, implies that to Foyn woman's place was definitely in the home, whereas his premodern wife had ideas reaching beyond darning socks and preparing meals. The divorce has echoes in local Texas lore, which hints that the tough, hard-slogging, fish-smelling seaman was overly friendly to brandy, something that was anathema to Elise. Whatever the nature of the incompatibility, they separated—but remained friends through their long lives, with Foyn occasionally sending money to help his onetime wife when she was in need, and Elise cherishing a certain admiration for her onetime husband.

But America, emigration, and notably Texas, rather than the early years in Norway, furnish the focus and area of central interest in the career of Elise Wærenskjold. She was influenced, as Dr. Clausen points out, by the dynamic Johan R. Reiersen, crusading reformer, newspaper editor, and proponent of emigration. In 1845 this liberal champion of the common people launched (with his brother Christian) a monthly magazine ("Norway and America") in which he published letters, reports, and articles extolling emigration, with special reference to Texas. In fact, Reiersen himself left for Texas in 1845 and edited the magazine (published at Arendal, Norway) from America. The next year, 1846–47, Elise took over as editor, but in the late summer of 1847 she followed in Reiersen's footsteps. Evidently she was persuaded by Reiersen's views — and perhaps by the propaganda in the magazine. Both her parents were dead; she had no brothers or sisters; her marriage had been terminated and she had no children. Thus, save for friendships, she was without ties in Norway. She went to Texas in a party led by Wilhelm Wærenskjold, whom she married in 1848. He was hearty, ambitious, talented, volatile, and unpredictable; and he liked to write sentimental verses, one of which was entitled "A Norseman's Nostalgia."

Dr. Clausen, in his introduction, reviews Elise Wærenskjold's American career in informing detail, emphasizing her glowing enthusiasm for Texas and her readiness to spring to its defense and indeed to the defense of all America in the face of antiemigration sentiment in Norway and elsewhere. He also deals with her moral aversion to slavery, her interest in the history of the settlements of her countrymen in Texas, her love of reading, and her affectionate interest in her community. Many of her letters do not go much underneath the surface of neighborhood affairs, but Dr. Clausen includes in his introduction extracts from a revealing pre-Civil War "Confession of Faith," written by Elise for her sons — and in this document she voices some of her deep convictions. Thus she records her view of slavery as an "abomination" contrary to the will of God. She brushes aside specious arguments for slavery based upon Bible texts, and she does it with shrewd reasoning. A revealing comment, suggestive of some divergence between her views and those of neighbors, is her reply to people who wondered if she would accept a Negro woman as a daughter-in-law. This, she said, would not please her "very much," but, she added, "I would rather have it thus than to have grandchildren who are slaves." Slavery itself would come to an end, for "institutions founded on injustice cannot survive." After the war, she expressed gratification that her sons had been too young to fight. "I would rather have left Texas a beggar," she wrote, "than have had my children fight to preserve slavery." In the "Confession of Faith," she also voices independent views on religious matters — rejecting, for

instance, the doctrine of the Trinity. But the private doubts she enter-
tained did not diminish the zeal with which she supported a church
and pastor for her community.

Mrs. Wærenskjold's interest in the Texas settlements is attested in
an early historical essay that she wrote for a Wisconsin magazine.
This is presented by Dr. Clausen under the title "A New Home in
America." There is evidence that in her later years she was interested
in the preparation of a history of the Texas Norwegian settlements.
It seems doubtful that she wrote one, but if she did, it has not come
to light. She knew the settlements at first hand and watched their
development through nearly five decades. As her letters reveal, she
traveled much in the several communities and was everywhere a welcome guest. In her own home and on her travels, she frequently
penned letters for her friends. According to local lore, she was a
"traveling newspaper,." And that lore also indicates a certain stateli-
ness in her bearing—wherever she went she was received "like a
bishop." Her hospitality accorded with the generous immigrant traditions of Lars Larsen in the days of the "sloopers" and of Even Heg
of Muskego fame. In a later letter, reviewing early times, she wrote,
"All the newcomers came directly to our house and stopped several
days, or weeks, with us—one family even stayed six months."

Life for Elise had its ups and downs. Some of her husband's ambitious plans—he tried both milling and farming—did not turn out
very well. The letters record passing scenes and events in faithful
detail. She writes of cotton, tobacco, and other crops; cattle; grasshopper plagues and drouth; land prices; church and community
affairs; friendships and simple pleasures; a book club that had sixteen
families enrolled (as early as 1857). She chronicles neighborhood ill-
nesses and the death of one of her three sons. There is a gap in the
letters for the Civil War years, but shortly afterward, Elise reviewed
the period and its problems in an interesting analytical survey.
Troubles did not end with the war, for in 1866 tragedy struck the
family. Elise's husband was stabbed to death in a cowardly assault
by an American neighbor. The murderer took off on his horse and
was not brought to justice until nearly a decade later. Dr. Clausen,
aided by newly discovered records of the trial, disposes once and for
all of the legend that the murder was occasioned by a dispute over

slavery. It seems clear that the quarrel was highly personal, though its precise reasons are not made clear in the trial records. Mrs. Wæren-skjold makes only sparing reference to the crime and the trial, but she does voice her opinion that the punishment (ten years in prison) was light. The crime, she wrote, was "cold-blooded and long premedi-tated" and the criminal "a scoundrel of a Methodist preacher." Some mystery envelops the story, but one stark fact emerges: the "lady with the pen" was a widow from 1866 until her death in 1895.

Many decades have passed since the years when Elise Wærenskjold lived at Four Mile Prairie, but she has not been forgotten in Texas. In the spring of 1959, I was guided through the communities where she lived by Mrs. Henry J. Gould of Fort Worth (Elise's great-granddaughter), saw the house where Mrs. Wærenskjold resided at Hamilton in her final years, visited the hamlet of "Norse," Prairie-ville, the interesting Bosque Memorial Museum at Clifton, and stopped in at various country homes. Everywhere the mention of Elise Wærenskjold was greeted with lively interest. Family lore was recounted and little episodes reported which, in sum total, impressed me with the unusual impact Elise had had in her home community. She was remembered as a woman of culture, of books and letter-writing; one of her paintings is owned by a grandson in Cleburne; a dozen or more of her letters have turned up in the neighborhood; and anecdotes about her have survived. One comment — a trifle unex-pected in view of the gentleness that characterizes most of the letters — was that she had a very sharp tongue and commanded a store of earthy epithets for occasional use. Her actions sometimes were brusque. Money used for jewelry, she thought, might better be spent for starving people abroad. As an older woman she wrote evening after evening by lamplight, without the aid of glasses.

She is remembered as a woman of dignity, of small stature, of strength and vigor. She had widely spaced eyes, a look of sharp alertness. Her pictures reveal her as dressed modestly but with good taste in the style of the time. Her hair had a center parting and in the portraits she wears a beribboned lace cap. In one picture a Norwegian breast pin appears on her embroidered collar. In the portrait from her later years she has an air of serenity, a faint and slightly quizzical smile — in eyes and on her lips.

She was greatly respected and indeed was, as Estelle G. Nelson has written, "A first lady of Texas." At her home many religious services and other gatherings were held, people coming by "ox cart, afoot, or by horseback, prepared to spend the day." Mrs. Nelson speaks of picnic lunches provided for such occasions: "jerked beef, roasted prairie hen, meal cakes (corn pones), cheese, wild berry jam, coffee, and mead." In the community I noted proud recognition of the fact that Mrs. Wærenskjold had won fame in wider circles through her career in Norway, her newspaper and magazine articles, and the tribute paid her by Rasmus B. Anderson in his *First Chapter of Norwegian Immigration*, published in 1895. He devoted a section to her career and described her as a "gifted, scholarly, kind, brave and noble woman."

From the letters, the "Confession of Faith," the newspaper and magazine pieces, cherished memories in Texas, and Dr. Clausen's introductory appraisal of her career, Elise Wærenskjold, as it seems to me, comes to life with dramatic vividness in the pages of this book. She has a secure, if modest, place in the pioneer history of Texas, as indeed she has in the larger saga of Norwegian immigration to America. She is also of historical interest in the domain of cultural interrelations between her homeland and the New World to which she came. As the panorama of events was unwound from the 1840's to the 1890's, she was a careful observer of things large and small. Some curious gaps there are, such as her singular lack of interest in American politics and literature — but she did not fail to speak out on the major American question, slavery, during the early decades of her immigrant experience. Her interest in and affection for Texas were never-ending, as was her concern for the settlements she helped to build and whose history she recorded. In drawing together and interpreting the letters and other records of the "Lady with the Pen," Dr. Clausen has contributed a volume of lasting interest.

*   *   *   *   *   *   *   *   *   *

This book has been a long time a-borning, and it represents much co-operative effort. Dr. Clausen indicates aid from various sources, but at his request I am recording yet other aids that have enhanced the interest and value of the work. Fundamental were the discovery and publication of many of Mrs. Wærenskjold's letters by Mr. Emil

Olsen, a Norwegian local historian who printed them in the newspaper *Tønsbergs blad* from May 11 to 26, 1925. These letters from
Elise to friends in Norway supply the framework of the volume. The
task of translating them along with other items — including the historical review written by Mrs. Wærenskjold for *Billed-magazin*, was
enthusiastically undertaken by the members of the Verdandi Study
Club of Minneapolis as a co-operative venture. In addition to translating the letters, the society later contributed toward the publication
of this book the sum of $100 as a memorial to Martha C. Blegen, a
member who had taken an active part in the work. A few years ago
I prepared a selection of Wærenskjold letters for a chapter in *Land of
Their Choice*, and Dr. Borge Madsen, now on the faculty of the
University of California, aided me in checking the earlier documents
and also in translating many additional letters that had come to light
— and these materials were made available for the present book. Dr.
Clausen has added yet other translations as further letters accumulated, and he has gone over the entire collection, revising the texts
that were placed in his hands.

My own thought of the possible publication of the Wærenskjold
letters as part of a large collection of America letters goes back to the
time when I was writing the first volume of *Norwegian Migration to
America*, issued in 1931. This plan necessarily was postponed, but it
was with the purpose of clearing the way for a special Wærenskjold
book that I asked the Verdandi Club, which had already aided the
Norwegian-American Historical Association in several earlier publications, for assistance in the work of translation. At the same time (1952)
I wrote Dr. Arne Odd Johnsen of Oslo, asking him to gather up all
possible information about Elise's career in Norway. The result was a
collection of detailed notes which later were turned over to Dr. Clausen
for his use. Dr. Johnsen also made transcripts for me of a series of elev-
en manuscript letters of Mrs. Wærenskjold which were presented to
the Norwegian-American Historical Association in 1929 by Oscar
Severson of Dallas, Texas, nephew of Wilhelm Wærenskjold. We have
also consulted Dr. Ingrid Gaustad Semmingsen, the leading Norwegian historian of emigration, and it may be added that Dr. Semmingsen includes in her distinguished two-volume work, *Veien mot
vest*, an excellent account of Mrs. Wærenskjold. Some of the letters in

the present volume were found in Norwegian-American newspapers by Dr. Carlton C. Qualey of Carleton College while doing research for his *Norwegian Settlement in the United States*, and photostats of these were secured.

Few of those who aided us have demonstrated a more lively and sustained interest than Mrs. Henry J. Gould of Fort Worth and Mr. Derwood Johnson of Waco. Jointly they made a major discovery — that of the district court records relating to the trial of the murderer of Elise's husband. This was an exciting adventure, the success of which was due to their Holmesian pursuit of clues and a fine unwillingness to abandon the search even after they had just about exhausted all the possibilities. Both Mrs. Gould and Mr. Johnson have helped in many other ways. I personally owe a debt to Mrs. Gould, whose hospitality and assistance were invaluable when I visited the old Texas settlements in 1959. In letter after letter she has sent on to us every item of information that she has unearthed in her relentless search — and Mr. Johnson has been equally energetic and helpful. Even all this assistance is not the whole story, for Mr. and Mrs. Gould matched the gift of the Verdandi Club, as a further contribution toward the cost of publishing the book. Many other friends in Texas gave generous help, including Mrs. Estelle G. Nelson, whose charmingly written pamphlet, *A First Lady of Texas*, I have taken the liberty of quoting in this foreword. Four years ago Mrs. Nelson gave me much initial help when I was attempting to get in touch with people in Texas who might furnish information about Mrs. Wærenskjold.

This publication bridges the period from my managing editorship to that of my successor, Dr. Kenneth O. Bjork. He took over editorial responsibility for the volume in midstream, so to speak, and he has given it patient care and effort in its later phases. Assisting him (and me) at every stage has been Helen Thane Katz, a veteran in the publication work of the association. Not only has she worked with complex problems of editing, with its multitude of details, including the identification of persons mentioned in the text as well as the task of indexing, but she even spent part of a vacation familiarizing herself with the locale of the story. Like myself she was guided to the Norwegian settlements in Texas by the indefatigable Lorena Gould.

I record finally the services of Dr. Clausen, who gladly acquiesced when I asked him to edit the book. He revised translations, arranged the letters, supplied them and the chapters with headings, wrote the historical and biographical introduction, and added explanatory footnotes on many points of special interest.

To those here mentioned and to all others who have made letters or pictures available or in other ways have contributed to the preparation and publication of *The Lady with the Pen*, I offer cordial thanks on behalf of the Norwegian-American Historical Association, plus my personal appreciation of good work done in a good cause.

Let me add a closing thought. It is highly probable that many of Elise's letters to Norway and to friends of hers in this country have not yet been found. I should like to invite readers of the book who have knowledge of letters or articles by Mrs. Wærenskjold that do not appear in these pages to inform the Norwegian-American Historical Association of the whereabouts of such materials. The association would be glad to receive the originals or to have photostats or microfilms made of them.

UNIVERSITY OF MINNESOTA   THEODORE C. BLEGEN
MINNEAPOLIS

Acknowledgments

In my work as editor of Elise Wærenskjold's letters, I have become indebted to many people. Dean Theodore C. Blegen, in addition to asking me to undertake this project and gathering invaluable materials for it over an extended period, has offered helpful suggestions along the way and acted as goad by setting numerous deadlines, most of which I failed to meet. My colleague, Professor Kenneth O. Bjork, as managing editor of the Norwegian-American Historical Association, has labored patiently and valiantly to prepare the manuscript for the press. Mr. Derwood Johnson of Waco, Texas, has served as an indispensable "resource man" on data connected with the Norwegian settlements in his state. His persistent detective work cleared up most of the problems surrounding the death of Wilhelm Wærenskjold.

Miss Karen Larsen deciphered several documents which were wrapped in the mysteries of German script, the most important being Mrs. Wærenskjold's "Confession of Faith," which threw a bright light on the author's religious philosophy. Many facts about the Tvede family and their circle were gleaned from notes prepared by Knut Bjørngaard of Oslo. Lloyd Hustvedt and Oivind Hovde sent me valuable material from archives in the State Historical Society of Wisconsin and in Luther College, respectively. Miss Dorothy Divers of the St. Olaf College art department designed the book's cover. Miss Carol Baumann, a student at St. Olaf, prepared the map used for the end sheets. The Texas State Historical Association supplied information on the areas of Norwegian settlement incorporated in the map and in several biographical items. Mrs. Mathilde Houkom and Miss Miriam Peterson have helped with the typing and collating. My wife, Marian B. Clausen, has been a consistent collaborator throughout and should by rights be listed as coeditor. To all of them I express my deepest gratitude.

C. A. CLAUSEN

ST. OLAF COLLEGE
NORTHFIELD, MINNESOTA

Contents

The Lady with the Pen

Introduction

C. A. Clausen

The fifteen-year interval between the annexation of Texas and the outbreak of the Civil War covered an expansive period in the history of the state. Settlers from other parts of the Union and from many foreign countries, attracted by liberal land offers, converged upon its plains to swell the population from about 100,000 in 1845 to more than 600,000 in 1860. Johan Reinert Reiersen, the most ardent champion of emigration in Norway during the forties, made a valiant effort to induce his countrymen to choose Texas rather than the Northwest areas as their home. Encouraged by General Sam Houston himself, Reiersen launched a propaganda campaign in his homeland and in 1845 founded a settlement in northeastern Texas with the challenging name of Normandy. Two years later, this first venture having proved somewhat disappointing, he went to an area now in Van Zandt and Kaufman counties, southeast of Dallas, and there founded a second settlement on Four Mile Prairie. These colonies did not develop to realize their founder's optimistic dreams, but in the history of Norwegian immigration they have won a place far more important than their size and wealth warrant, a result in no small measure due to letters and articles from the facile pen of Elise Amalie Tvede Wærenskjold.[1]

[1] Texas was admitted to the Union in December, 1845. Discussions of Norwegian settlement in Texas are found in Theodore C. Blegen, *Norwegian Migration to America, 1825–1860,* 177–189 (Northfield, Minnesota, 1931); Carlton C. Qualey, *Norwegian Settlement in the United States,* 198–209 (Northfield, 1938); Rasmus B. Anderson, *First Chapter of Norwegian Immigration (1821–1840): Its Causes and*

Elise Tvede was born February 19, 1815, in Dypvåg parsonage, Kristiansand diocese, where her father, Nicolai (Niels) Seiersløv Tvede, was then serving as pastor.[2] Through him she was related to the famous Aall family, which was very influential in Norway during the early nineteenth century. Members of this group were prominent in industrial and commercial life, but they are still better known for the part they played in 1814, when Norway declared her independence of Denmark and drew up her present constitution. Two Aall brothers, Jacob and Jørgen, were "Eidsvoldsmenn" who helped frame the constitution, while a third, Niels, served in the first Norwegian cabinet and was later sent to England to try to win support for the young nation. The ties between the Tvedes and the Aalls were much closer than the mere family relationship would indicate. Jacob Aall was best man at Nicolai Tvede's wedding, while Mrs. Jacob Aall acted as one of five sponsors at Elise's baptism. Jacob Aall, who married Lovise Andrea Stephansen, a cousin of Pastor Tvede, had come to know the Stephansen and Tvede families while he was a student in Copenhagen, and he may have been instrumental in bringing the young pastor to Dypvåg.[3] Elise's parents, like many people who held official positions in Norway during the long political union with Denmark that began in 1380, were Danish born, but they seem to have become thoroughly Norwegian in sympathies and interests. The times they lived in were stirring ones, both politically

Results, 370–395 (Madison, Wisconsin, 1896); Ingrid Semmingsen, *Veien mot vest: Utvandringen fra Norge til Amerika, 1825–1865*, 276–283 (Oslo, 1942); Johan R. Reiersen, *Veiviser for norske emigranter til de forenede nordamerikanske stater og Texas*, chapter 9 (Guide for Norwegian Emigrants to the United North American States and Texas — Christiania, 1844). Copies of Reiersen's book are in the Minnesota Historical Society and at Luther College, Decorah, Iowa. Chapter 9 has been translated by Derwood Johnson of Waco, Texas, and will appear in volume 21 of *Norwegian-American Studies and Records*. Selections from Elise Wærenskjold's letters are in Theodore C. Blegen, ed., *Land of Their Choice: The Immigrants Write Home*, 321–350 (Minneapolis, 1955). The name Christiania was changed to Oslo in 1925.

[2] Pastor Tvede was appointed to a chaplaincy in Holt Parish in 1806. He later served three parishes in the Kristiansand diocese — Dypvåg, West Moland, and Holt — where he died in 1832. His daughter gave the name Niels to her second son. Elise's mother, Johanne Elisabeth Meldahl Tvede, died in 1839.

[3] Elise said in one of her letters, "Old Jacob Aall's wife was my father's cousin, and since his parents died while he was a child, they [*the cousins*] were brought up together and thought of each other as brother and sister." Jacob Aall's *Erindringer som bidrag til norges historie fra 1800–1815* (Memoirs as a Contribution to Norwegian History from 1800 to 1815—Christiania, 1844–45) ranks high in the historical literature of Norway, and his translation from Old Norse, *Snorre Sturlesons norske kongers sagaer* (Sagas of the Kings of Norway—Christiania, 1838–39) became a real *folkebok*.

and intellectually, and apparently their daughter absorbed many of her ideas and ideals from her parents, especially her father.

Nicolai Tvede was active in community affairs. He did much to systematize poor relief in the parishes he served, something sorely needed during the "bark bread days" of the war years, 1807–14, and the depression that followed the collapse of Napoleon. Apparently Tvede had a lively interest in agriculture and made many improvements on the parish glebe (*prestegård*). In his day there was a great awakening of interest in popular education, especially among the pastors, who usually served as chairmen of the district school boards. After the war ended, a resident teacher was employed for Holt Parish, where Tvede later served as pastor, and it is interesting that the first man to fill this position was Ole Reiersen, the sexton, father of Johan Reinert Reiersen. After 1816 the busy pastor had additional opportunity to serve his district, as he was appointed to the conciliation council.[4] He is, moreover, credited with having prepared "excellent census lists" for his parishes, which have provided invaluable data for later students.

The verdict of a parish historian may be indicative of Pastor Tvede's talents and interests: he "formed in many respects a contrast to his predecessor, whom he surpassed in gifts and secular abilities but whose inferior he was as a theologian and preacher."[5] He seems to have been typical of the Dano-Norwegian pastors who were educated at the University of Copenhagen during the flowering period of rationalism, or the Enlightenment, at that institution from about 1750 to 1800. Later generations have jokingly or derisively referred to some of these pastors as "potato priests" (*potetprester*) because of their enthusiastic propaganda for that highly productive vegetable when hunger and famine frequently stalked the land. They saw the potato as a godsend for the nation, especially for the poverty-stricken cotters and peasants, who usually tried to drown their misery in quantities of cheap but potent liquor. It was said that one potato priest, in his enthusiasm, exclaimed from the pulpit, "And hast thou

[4] Conciliation councils (*forlikelseskommisjoner*) are found in all rural and urban districts in Norway. Before a suit can be brought into court, the parties to the disagreement must endeavor to reach a settlement by bringing their case to the local council.

[5] Andreas Faye, *Bidrag til Holts presters og prestegjelds historie*, 88 (Arendal, Norway, 1859).

a field which slopes toward the south, verily, I say unto thee, plant potatoes!"; and that another closed his sermon by asserting that there would be divine services again in two weeks, God willing, "And furthermore, it can be announced that if anyone needs potatoes for planting and little pigs for rearing, such can be had at the parsonage."

In the Norwegian church, rationalism was strongest precisely during Pastor Tvede's time and in the diocese where he served. But even though he seems to have been inspired by the rationalistic enthusiasm for material progress, education, and virtue, he was probably not a full-blown rationalist in theology; rather he seems to have been a follower of the famous Danish bishop of Zealand, Nicolai Edinger Balle, who, though by no means uninfluenced by the Enlightenment, "stood immovably firm as the defender of the Bible and Christianity." [6] Tvede introduced Balle's controversial textbook (*Lærebog*) on religion in his parish almost immediately after taking office, substituting it for the pietistic and thoroughly orthodox epitome (*Lille forklaring*) by Bishop Pontoppidan.

As has been indicated, Elise Tvede's attitude toward life seems to have been deeply influenced by her father. We shall see later that she was mildly rationalistic in her religious views and, throughout a long life, a tireless champion of advanced causes. In Norway she is still remembered as a woman leader (*foregangskvinne*), because she refused to be confined within the narrow bounds which at that time circumscribed the activities of her sex. We know nothing specifically about her childhood years except that long afterward (in 1892) in faraway Texas, she referred to them as the happiest of her life and asked wistfully about the beautiful garden at Møglestue. Like other girls of her station, she was probably educated at home by her parents and by private tutors. She acquired a good command of English, French, and German, and developed some skill in painting. Though she never assumed any musical knowledge, she probably had voice and piano lessons; such training was usual among people of quality (*kondisjonerte*).[7]

<hr/>

[6] Hal Koch, *Danmarks kyrka genom tiderna*, 128 (Stockholm, 1942).

[7] Four water-color paintings formerly owned by Elise, one done by her, are in the possession of Otto M. Warenskjold of Cleburne, Texas, her grandson. The term *kondisjonerte* was applied to the official classes, who usually were well educated and had

At nineteen, two years after Nicolai Tvede's death, Elise took the unusual step — for a woman — of becoming a schoolteacher, first in Tønsberg and later in Lillesand, where she decided to open a handicraft school for girls. This was intended to be supported by private means, but she hoped that the public schools would furnish free quarters. When she presented her plan to the mayor, she was curtly informed that a woman was presumptuous to advance such a public undertaking. Nothing daunted, Elise persisted; the school she managed to set up was so successful that it continued to function even after she left for America.[8]

But the cause to which she gave her most ardent support in the 1840's was probably the temperance movement. Since about 1770 the consumption of brandy had become an evil that threatened the very fiber of the Scandinavian nations.[9] These were the decades that elevated the drinking song to a literary genre. Poets as different as the stern orthodox bishop of Bergen, Johan Nordahl Brun, and that charming scapegrace, Karl Michael Bellman, sang the praises of the grape and of the "cellar nymphs" who dispensed it. All classes of society were affected, but the worst victims were undoubtedly the small farmers, who, in home distilling, found a method of transforming cumbersome grain into a product small in bulk and much in demand. Originally no stigma was attached to this activity. "The clergymen who lived on glebe lands and took their fees in kind, of course, operated their own stills and often ranked among the larger, privileged producers."[10] Even as late as 1836 the highly respected Jacob Aall, writing the necrology of his brother-in-law, Niels Seiersløv Stephansen, praised him for his conservative religious

traveled extensively. They formed an upper class, replacing the hereditary nobility, which was abolished in 1821. Toward the end of the nineteenth century, with the rapid development of democracy and industrialism, the official group lost its social and political pre-eminence.

[8] Hartvig Johnsen, *Elise Tvede: En norsk foregangskvinne i kampen mot alkoholen*, 6 (Oslo, 1944).

[9] The heavy drinking of the time was not, of course, confined to the Scandinavian countries. Neither Germany nor the United States escaped, and the insobriety of the British became notorious. "It is safe to say that drinking [in the United States] was almost universal, among women as well as men, and that public drunkenness, at least for men, was no disgrace. Even ministers were apt to exhibit a degree of conviviality at ordination ceremonies, conferences, and college commencements that later generations would have regarded with astonishment." John D. Hicks, *The Federal Union: A History of the United States to 1865*, 489 (Boston, 1937).

[10] Brynjolf J. Hovde, *The Scandinavian Countries, 1720–1865: The Rise of the Middle Classes*, 2:665 (Ithaca, New York, 1948).

views and his beneficent community leadership, adding that the good pastor early thought of combining distilling with his other activities and even constructed a building for it and procured the necessary apparatus. He abandoned the project, however, partly because he had concluded that a small-scale distillery would not net the anticipated income and partly because he questioned the moral influence that the enterprise might have on his parishioners.[11]

By this time, however, a strong reaction against the drinking evil had set in. Champions of temperance, both lay and clerical, had begun their agitation in most parts of the country. At first, Elise Tvede was not much impressed, feeling that the propagandists were inspired by a futile hope. But in 1841 Pastor Jakob F. Fridrichsen and other leading citizens organized a temperance society for Lillesand and its environs that permitted moderate use of punch but demanded total abstinence from such strong drinks as brandy, toddy, and grog. Elise then began to take the movement seriously; she noticed that, contrary to her expectations, many people proved willing to observe the restrictions. Once convinced of the temperance society's efficacy, she joined it — the first woman to do so. "The fact that no women in our community had as yet become members of the society was no longer any deterrent for me but rather a potent motive for joining," she explained later.[12] At the same time she issued an appeal to other women; this, plus her example, evidently carried weight, because soon it became common practice for members of her sex to affiliate with the movement.[13]

Having espoused the cause, Elise Tvede threw herself into the work enthusiastically. In 1843 she published a pamphlet with the awesome title, "Summons to All Noble Men and Women to Unite in Temperance Societies for the Purpose of Eradicating Drunkenness and the Use of Brandy, Together with a Brief Exposition of the Deleterious Effects of Brandy Drinking." Later she published an article in a temperance magazine in which she urged her fellow

---

[11] Jacob Aall, *Nutid og fortid: Et hæfteskrift*, vol. 2, part 2–3, p. 272 (Arendal, 1834). Niels Seiersløv Stephansen, Mrs. Aall's brother, was a cousin of Nicolai Seiersløv Tvede, Elise's father.

[12] From an unsigned article by Elise Tvede in *Maadeholds-tidende* (Christiania), no. 19, p. 145–152 (1845). The piece was entitled "Om maadeholdssagen" (About the Temperance Movement), and was signed, "Af en Dame" (By a Lady).

[13] Hartvig Johnsen, *Elise Tvede*, 8.

citizens to join the crusade against the national evil. These were probably the first temperance appeals published by any woman in Norway; she has an honored place in the annals of the movement.[14]

"It is one of the crying needs of our time, but also one of the most difficult undertakings," she wrote in an article, "to put a stop tc the disastrous liquor consumption." She pointed out that restrictive laws were ineffective; taxes had failed to reduce drinking; equally futile had been the most fervent admonitions on the part of religious leaders. Only an aroused public opinion and a general rally to the support of the temperance societies would bring results, she argued. And she continued by saying that no reform of any kind could be achieved without the support of the women. Therefore they should abjure the evil themselves, give up their resistance to the societies, and by their own example do everything in their power to further this common cause.

She did not confine herself to words. Early in 1843 she contributed 14 *spesiedaler* to the society for the purchase of temperance literature, to be distributed free, or sold; and in November of that year she wrote Pastor Fridrichsen, chairman of the society, that she had drawn up her will, setting aside 400 *spesiedaler* for the benefit of worthy members, men or women, who could not qualify for public relief. The interest was not to be used until after her death, but since this might involve a long delay — she was twenty-eight at

[14] The pamphlet, entitled *Opfordring til alle ædle mænd og quinder* . . . , was published in Kristiansand in 1843. On the article, see footnote 12. Mrs. Henry J. Gould of Fort Worth, Texas, a great-granddaughter of Elise Wærenskjold, has furnished a handwritten copy of the pamphlet. It is neatly and legibly made, evidently by the author herself, and runs to 43 pages. Among the sources cited in the pamphlet is Robert Baird, *Histoire des Sociétés de Temperance des États Unis d' Amérique* (Paris, 1836). Baird was an American, but the original edition appeared in French; later it was translated into other languages. Charles XIV John, king of Norway-Sweden (1818–44), was so impressed with the book that he had it translated into Swedish and distributed at his own expense. Charles John's gracious successor, Oscar I, also worked for temperance, but at least one observer, the Swedish poet H. B. Palmer, seemed to be skeptical of the results:

> Kung Oskar sitter på Stockholms slott
> Och nickar och nickar och nickar.
> Kring honom står hans forsupna folk
> Och hickar och hickar och hickar.

> (King Oscar sits in the Stockholm palace
> And nods, and nods, and nods.
> Around him stand his drunken subjects
> And hic, and hic, and hic.)

the time — she offered to make the equivalent of 4 per cent available for distribution by January 1, 1844.

Evidence of the restricted economic conditions of the time appears in the method of distributing the fund the first year:

"1. Shoemaker Johan Sørensen was granted an interest-free loan of 5 *spesiedaler* to buy material for shoes, the sum to be repaid in five annual installments of 1 *spesiedaler* each.

"2. Thorbjørn Mortensen was granted a gift of 4 *spesiedaler* for the purchase of fishing equipment.

"3. Schoolteacher M. R. Riis was granted 3½ *spesiedaler* for the purchase of an arithmetic text and a set of copybooks, as well as pens, paper, and slate pencils to be sold.

"4. Christian Guttormsen Humlesund was granted 3½ *spesiedaler* for the purchase of a boat and fishing tackle or of the necessary clothes, in case he got a job at the opening of the shipping season." [15]

It is easily understood that beneficiaries such as these listened eagerly to accounts about America and, during the following decades, crossed the "dam" (as the Atlantic was called) by the thousands to seek a more abundant life.

Elise Tvede, besides being known in Norway as a *foregangskvinne*, is also remembered as the first wife of Svend Foyn, who later became an economic giant and accumulated a vast fortune. "Like no one else, he broke new paths and created an entirely new livelihood for his country. His life and his work have even taken on world dimensions, since the whole modern whaling industry builds on his inventions and industry." [16] His was a success story without parallel in Norwegian history. But when Elise Tvede married him in 1839 he was a struggling young sea captain possessed of little but an indomitable determination to get ahead. His occupation forced him to spend most of his time away from home, and the young couple developed few common interests to serve as bonds between them. Gradually they realized that they were not suited to each other; in 1842 they took the then daring step of separating — on her initiative, it is said. [17] It is interesting to note that when this independent

[15] Hartvig Johnsen, *Elise Tvede*, 9–11.
[16] Sigurd Risting, "Svend Foyn," in *Norsk biografisk leksikon*, 4:215 (Oslo, 1929). See also Arne Odd Johnsen, *Svend Foyn og hans dagbog* (Oslo, 1943).
[17] Though the separation took place in 1842, the divorce was not legally completed until January 10, 1849, several months after Elise's marriage to Wærenskjold in Texas.

couple got married, they neglected to have the banns read, contrary to the almost universal practice of the time.

Elise, commenting many years later (1894) on the separation, said, "Due to incompatibility — absolutely nothing else — we agreed to a friendly separation, and he has truly proved to be a friend by sending me money on several occasions." According to one account, Foyn was critical of his wife's many independent activities; besides, he directed her attention to work more suited to her and her position in life, namely "to iron my shirts and darn my socks."[18]

Be that as it may, anyone who studies the temperaments of the two individuals will realize that they were indeed incompatible. Both were strong personalities and had minds and interests of their own. Foyn's resoluteness and stubbornness have become legendary: "His will was adamant. He did not tolerate any opposition. If he was contradicted this usually led to a break. He was a man of stern temperament who would permit no circumstances to deflect him from his purpose."[19] The famous author, Jonas Lie, quotes the seamen as saying that Foyn did not have the patience to let his subordinates develop their abilities; everything, to the most minute detail, had to be carried out so completely according to his ideas that there was no need for anyone else to have a head.[20] This must have led inevitably to disagreements with his wife, for her head was a very good one and she was determined to use it. Furthermore, Foyn's interests were very narrow. Outside of his work and his religion, few things attracted him. "Consequently there was always something cramped about him." With the husband's activities becoming more and more restricted, and the wife's ever broader, it was natural that the two should go their separate ways.

But to the end of her days Elise continued to follow the strange

---

Presumably she was unaware, when she remarried, that the divorce action was not final. Derwood Johnson, an attorney of Waco, Texas, states, in a letter to the editor, July 21, 1959, "One of the . . . old-timers of Bosque County told me that Wilhelm W. was a bookkeeper for Foyn in Norway and that the bookkeeper had stolen Foyn's wife. This is, of course, hearsay." Correspondence and other unpublished material, the location of which is not specifically mentioned, has been filed in the archives of the Norwegian-American Historical Association at Northfield, Minnesota.

[18] S. Hageland, "Elise Tvede: En foregangskvinde i Lillesand for 80 aar siden," in *Lillesands-posten*, December 28, 1922.

[19] Risting, in *Norsk biografisk leksikon*, 4:219.

[20] Jonas Lie, "Svend Foyn og ishavsfarten," in *Samlede værker: Mindeudgave*, 3:343 (Christiania, 1909).

career of the iron man to whom she had been linked for some three years. She could not love him, but obviously she admired him. Once, being in dire financial straits, she wrote him explaining her situation. "And, just think, he was so extremely kind as to send me $400! There is perhaps not one man in a thousand — no, hardly one in a million — who would have done as much for a divorced wife as Foyn has done for me. I was so happy I slept very little that night." In 1889, when she was seventy-four, she wrote to a friend in Norway, "I wonder if Svend Foyn is going whaling again; he will be eighty in June. Can one buy a picture of him?"

After the separation, Elise Tvede resumed her maiden name, and in 1846 we find her in Christiania as editor of Christian and Johan Reinert Reiersen's monthly periodical, *Norge og Amerika*, which had been launched the year before. We do not know how she became involved in this venture, but she must have been acquainted with the Reiersens since childhood days, because, as has been indicated, their father served as sexton and schoolteacher in one of Pastor Tvede's parishes. Since Johan's birth in 1810, he had managed to accumulate considerable experience and a controversial reputation. He had been a private tutor; had been expelled from the university "for some youthful indiscretion"; had traveled on the Continent; had founded *Christianssandsposten*, "through which he worked for education, religious tolerance, and the development of public sentiment, doing all he could to promote liberty and independence" and had fought the intemperance evil with all his might, acquiring the nickname "the apostle of temperance." If we add to all this the fact that "he often criticised the officeholding class, and was always ready to take the part of the poor against the abuses of those in power," we can understand why he became a target for conservative editors, most especially Adolph Stabell, the editor of *Morgenbladet*, Norway's leading newspaper at the time.[21]

A crusader of this type would naturally attract a public-spirited person like Elise Tvede, and undoubtedly common interests were what brought them together. When Reiersen set off for Texas with his first group of emigrants, she assumed the editorship of *Norge og*

---

[21] Anderson, *Norwegian Immigration*, 370–372, 374. There is a partial file of *Norge og Amerika* (Arendal, Norway) at Luther College.

Amerika, whose purpose was to acquaint the people of Norway with conditions in the New World and thus promote emigration. Reiersen believed it essential to find new homes for the thousands of his countrymen "then gathering crumbs from the table of the aristocracy." This naturally gave him further incentive to agitate for liberal causes, for he believed America to be the land of human rights. It was unusual, if not unique, for Norwegian women to engage in journalism at that time, and visitors to the office were no little surprised when they discovered that the editor, E. Tvede, was a woman.

Norge og Amerika ceased publication in July, 1847, and that same year Elise Tvede, then thirty-two, left for Texas, arriving there in October, 1847. She had undoubtedly been attracted by the promise of the richer life, not least for a woman of her interests and talents, that America held forth to the people of the Old World.

Elise stopped in Nacogdoches and Brownsboro, Texas, then moved to Four Mile Prairie, in Van Zandt County, a few miles from Prairieville, in Kaufman County, where she married Wilhelm Wærenskjold, with whom she had crossed the Atlantic.[22] They acquired rights to a square mile of land, and soon this lady, delicately reared in her father's parsonage, became a sturdy prairie wife, entering wholeheartedly into the spirit of the agrarian frontier. "I have always had a liking for farm and country life," she wrote a friend in Norway in 1852, "and if one is otherwise happy in his position, I cannot imagine a more pleasant or more independent state, for in this country a tiller of the soil is respected as much as anyone else, be he official or merchant." She soon became acquainted with the mysteries of grain growing and cattle raising, and, like farmers eternally, worried about rainfall, insects, bankers, and market prices. She planned and labored eagerly to develop an orchard comparable to those she had known in the old land, and we can guess that her sister-in-law, who was contemplating emigration, felt like changing her plans when she received from Texas a request to bring along pits and slips of practically every type of fruit tree known to Norwegian horticulture.

[22] They were married September 10, 1848. They had three sons: Otto Christian Wilhelm, born May 5, 1851; Niels Seiersløv Tvede, December 12, 1853; Thorvald August, October 4, 1858. Wilhelm's parents were Lieutenant Otto Christian Wærenskjold and Cathrine Caroline Poulsen. The family was well known in both Denmark

The Wærenskjolds intended to go into stock raising on a rather large scale. By 1857 Elise could write: "We do not plan to sell the cows, just the steers, until we can acquire about two hundred calves a year. This spring we can expect about seventy. . . . We have sixty-two sheep, and this month and next we are expecting many lambs." Wilhelm was an active man who went into milling and contracting, as well as farming. He undoubtedly had big hopes for the future. But then came the Civil War and all the calamities that it brought to the South. There was scarcely any actual fighting on Texas soil, but nevertheless the war and the years following dealt a hard blow to Elise's dreams. During the next decades she frequently struggled with poverty, brought on by the hard times of the seventies and by such acts of God as drought and grasshopper invasions. To supplement farm income, she took on extra work: selling books, teaching school, and taking orders for magazine subscriptions and garden seed; and on at least one occasion, as we have seen, she made bold to ask Svend Foyn for aid.

Life might have been different had not Wilhelm been killed by a "scoundrel of a Methodist preacher" named N. T. Dickerson.[23] The facts surrounding this crime have long been unclear. Rasmus B. Anderson claimed that Wærenskjold was assassinated during the Civil War because he was a Northern sympathizer, whereas the murder took place November 17, 1866.[24] Elise, writing to her sister-in-law in November, 1865, said that she had recently written to a number of friends in Norway, and continued: "If Schjøth received my letter you will know how we lived during the war and that Wilhelm had

and Norway. The original Wærenskjold received that name when ennobled in 1697 by the king of Denmark-Norway. Wilhelm, whose full name was Johan Matheus Christian Wilhelm, was born in 1822; thus he was seven years younger than Elise. A genealogical table of the family was prepared by R. Wærenskjold about 1924; a blueprint of it was lent by Mrs. Francis Webb. On the land grants, see State of Texas, General Land Office, Austin, certificates, 1850–52; citation furnished by Derwood Johnson. Four Mile Prairie supposedly was so named because in width it was bounded by two streams that were four miles apart; information furnished by Mr. Roy Barzak of Waco, courtesy of Derwood Johnson. Wærenskjold served for a time as justice of the peace and, among other things, officiated at marriages.

[23] State of Texas vs. N. T. Dickerson, testimony of James Bowlden (and others), District Court Records, Kaufman County, Texas, Document No. 332, filed February 13, 1875; summary furnished by Derwood Johnson. Elise said definitely that Dickerson was a Methodist preacher; a witness at the trial stated that he "farmed some, hunted some, and coopered some," but the court record says nothing of his having been a minister. See Elise Wærenskjold to R. B. Anderson, July 3, 1895, in the present volume; Derwood Johnson, summary, Texas vs. N. T. Dickerson, p. 8.

[24] Anderson, *Norwegian Immigration*, 384.

some trouble as a result of the struggle. Fortunately, all this is over and done with now; he has completely regained his health and has obtained a small position which, however, pays him practically nothing." Unfortunately, the Schjøth letters have not been recovered and consequently we are left somewhat in the dark about Wilhelm's difficulties. But it seems unlikely that the slavery question or the Civil War had anything to do with the killing. No reference is made to disagreements over either matter as a motive for the crime in the documents filed in connection with the case. The quarrel seems to have been of a purely personal nature, the defendant's lawyers requesting the court to instruct the jury that the slaying was instigated by "insulting words or conduct of the person killed, towards a female relation of the party guilty of the homicide." [25]

It should be borne in mind that this was a turbulent era in the history of Texas. "The period between the close of the Civil War and the mid-nineties was productive of 'bad men' of all descriptions. The cattle trails, border disturbances and chiefly Reconstruction, all contributed their quota of gentlemen with notches on their guns." John Hardin and Sam Bass were undoubtedly the most notorious of the breed. "Race riots flared, the Ku Klux Klan rode, and lawlessness gripped the state as thousands of freed Negroes, cast adrift, congregated in towns and near military camps, existing by begging or by occasionally doing odd jobs." [26]

Dickerson was no Sam Bass. As a matter of fact, all the witnesses at the trial seemed to agree that he had a reputation for being a "quiet, peaceable man" and a nondrinker. Still, certain facets of the case reflect the age in which the murder occurred: in the first place, the cold-blooded manner in which this "peaceable" man had planned the crime. He engaged a blacksmith to make a big hunting knife for him after a wooden pattern and also had him repair his pistol. When these articles were ready, he vowed to "make them whoop for the landing," an expression used among hunters in search

[25] It is certain that the "troubles" were partly physical. In a letter of March 20, 1865, to Carl Quæstad, Wilhelm stated that his health was so poor that he had been forced to seek a doctor. A photostatic copy of this letter was sent to the editor by Derwood Johnson; the original is in the possession of Mrs. Ole J. Hoel of Norse, Texas. At the conclusion of the trial, "The court refused to charge the jury as requested by the defense counsel on the grounds that there was no evidence to support the charge." Derwood Johnson, summary, Texas vs. N. T. Dickerson, p. 14.

[26] *Texas: A Guide to the Lone Star State*, 49, 51 (New York, 1940).

of big game. But Dickerson evidently had some other quarry in mind, because he later told several of his neighbors that the next time he met Wærenskjold he was going to "hurt him and hurt bad, that he was prepared for him now." He opened his coat wide and showed the pistol strapped on one side of his body and the knife on the other. As one of the witnesses explained, "It was the custom to carry pistols; there was a great deal of lawlessness; the country was unsettled." Dickerson encountered Wærenskjold in James Bowlden's store and post office in Prairieville, stabbed him, and immediately fled from the neighborhood. Wærenskjold died almost instantly. Several warrants for Dickerson's arrest were issued during the years immediately following, but apparently no real search was made until the spring of 1874, when he was apprehended. The trial took place February 12, 1875. He was found guilty of second-degree murder and confined to the state penitentiary for ten years at hard labor.[27]

Elise felt that this was a very mild punishment for "such a cold-blooded and long-premeditated murder." The lawyers' fees and other expenses connected with the case were heavy burdens for her at a time when she was ill prepared to assume them. She may have had such costs in mind when some years later (1882) she complained, "Here we are ruined by doctors and lawyers."

Both Wilhelm and Elise Wærenskjold, on more than one occasion, defended the Americans against charges of lawlessness made by European observers, but did admit that their new fellow citizens were inspired by an excessive sense of honor which might lead to demands for bloody satisfaction. "In my opinion," Wilhelm Wærenskjold wrote in 1852, "such an excess must simply be regarded as a misconception of the way in which to maintain one's honor — a misconception that once animated the nobility and to some extent still prevails among the military in Europe."[28] In the same vein, Mrs. Wærenskjold wrote a few years later to her young sons: "The false sense of honor is the main cause of the frequent murders in this country. If a person is affronted or insulted he believes that for the sake of his honor he must seek revenge. Far sooner would he become

[27] The case was appealed, but the appeal must have been abandoned before its final determination. Elise Wærenskjold to Madam Staack, March 6, 1875, in the present volume; Derwood Johnson to the editor, May 22, 1959.

[28] Blegen, ed., *Land of Their Choice*, 355.

a murderer than be regarded as a coward. The judgment of God means nothing to him, the judgment of the world, everything. . . . I would assuredly mourn far more if one of you should die at the hands of a murderer than if God through a natural death should take one of you away from me; but sooner, far sooner, would I have you die a violent death than that you yourself should commit a murder, unless this was done in absolute self-defense." [29]

The slaying of Wilhelm Wærenskjold was naturally a great shock to his wife. But the reader of her letters is left with the impression that the relationship between the two was not especially warm. She admired his ability and his dexterity "at all kinds of work." He was evidently energetic and planned big for the future — too much so, it seems, to please her: "He spends about as much time there [*at the mill*] as at home, and this very evening he has undertaken a new job" — which would mean still more absences. His little vanities irritated her, as when he "got it into his head" that he would not ride in an oxcart. And even though he wrote sentimental immigrant poetry about his longing for his "ever-beloved North," it seemed to Elise, at least, that his passion for Norway was not as genuine as hers, and consequently she feared that they would never visit the beloved homeland again. She also confessed to her children that she wished her husband shared her faith in prayer, so that all of them could unite in brief family devotions every evening and in singing hymns and reading sermons on holidays. Despite the fact that Wilhelm was an educated man, he evidently did not take as intense an interest in the education and upbringing of their sons as she felt he should. "God only knows," she wrote impatiently, "how our husbands can be so indifferent toward a project [*the building of a school-house*] that is of so very great importance to our children. In a society where community spirit is lacking, nothing can thrive or prosper." To her great satisfaction, Wilhelm abstained from the use of strong drink and took a lead in organizing temperance societies

[29] This quotation is from a hand-written manuscript addressed by Elise "To My Dear and Fervently Beloved Children," which she refers to as her "Confession of Faith" (*Min religiøse troesbekjendelse*). Internal evidence indicates that this "Confession" was written after the birth of Thorvald, October 4, 1858, and before the outbreak of the Civil War. She intended each of her sons to have a copy. The one made for the Wærenskjolds' eldest son, Otto, has been examined by the editor through the courtesy of Mrs. Henry J. Gould. Transcribed, it runs to 28 pages.

in the settlement, but this did not prevent him from entering with great gusto into the spirit of parties and picnics. As early as 1852 the Norwegians on Four Mile Prairie were celebrating the Fourth of July "a good twenty-four hours." Wilhelm not only contributed half an ox and half a dollar as his share to make the festivities possible but he also was moved to give a speech. Mrs. Wærenskjold makes it plain that she felt the party was a bit too lusty, "but such things are just to Wilhelm's liking, especially when he can be at the head of the whole affair."

"My greatest joy is Otto," she says in the same paragraph, and here she touches upon the most profound element of her life: her love and concern for her children. Even when she wrote home of Wilhelm's death she referred to him as "the loving father of my children"; and she expressed deep anxiety lest she too be carried away before they were old enough to take care of themselves. The deepest sorrow of her life undoubtedly struck her when, early in 1866, her little Tulli (Thorvald) died, "the dearest thing we possessed on this earth."

The concern expressed in Elise Wærenskjold's letters about getting Lutheran pastors for the community and having her sons confirmed would naturally lead to the assumption that she was thoroughly orthodox. But in her "Confession of Faith" — which was written for her sons, and *only* for them, lest her ideas give offense to others — she divulged that she did not believe in the doctrine of the Trinity: "I believe that there is one God — not one God in three persons — but in reality and truth only one God, and that this God has been from everlasting and will remain throughout eternity; that he is possessed of the most noble and majestic attributes and that he in his sublimity embodies everything that we can imagine." But still she did not believe that Jesus Christ was a mere human being: "No! I conceive of him as a higher being, free of sin, sent us by God as our Saviour and atoner." That Christ was more than a human being was attested, she maintained, by the fact that his teachings were much more elevated and pure than those of other religious leaders. Mohammedanism, for instance, "degraded half of the human race, namely the women, to beings who existed only for the sake of the men. . . . This is a crime against nature and does violence to the natural feelings of right and wrong."

By a logical transition this led her to an examination of Mormonism, which she also found less than divine because, like Islam, in her opinion it debased women to an inferior position in society. She believed in the efficacy of faith but evidently not in "faith alone" because it was essential that "this faith should show its power through good deeds, through love of one's fellow men; otherwise it is a dead and sterile faith, of no worth in the sight of God." She accepted the Bible as the word of God, and the prophets and apostles as divinely inspired spokesmen, but "they expressed themselves in the manner of their nation and their age; therefore many things are so stated that they become obscure to us, and many poetic similes are taken literally by fanatics and consequently misunderstood, while the skeptics use such passages as targets for their blasphemies and witticisms." Without a belief in immortality, she felt, life would be miserable and meaningless. In the hereafter people would be rewarded or punished according to their deserts, but the eschatological language of the Bible should be taken figuratively, not literally. She did not accept the doctrine of predestination: "How could God be a just God if he created us such that we necessarily had to commit this or that vice, and later punished us for it?" The theory of evolution (evidently as expounded by the Norwegian pre-Darwinian, Professor Niels Treschow) she found "absolutely unacceptable and quite as contrary to sound reasoning as to the Bible." [30]

The discussion of religion led her to a consideration of the slavery question. Since it may be interesting to see what this immigrant woman had to say, on the eve of the Civil War, about "the peculiar institution," we shall quote her directly at some length.

"I believe that slavery is absolutely contrary to the law of God, because the law commands us to love God and our neighbors as ourselves, and, further, that whatsoever we want others to do unto us, that we should do toward them. These rules are as . . . easily understood as they are true. . . . Let us now ask ourselves if we would be satisfied with being slaves, with being sold like animals, with being separated from our mates and our children whenever it might suit our masters, with seeing our children brought up in thralldom and ignorance without the slightest possibility of rising above the miserable state into which we were born, despite the fact that we

[30] From her "Confession of Faith."

might have the highest abilities and the greatest eagerness to learn. To all this we must without qualification answer 'No!' — answer that it would make us immeasurably unhappy. Consequently slavery must be contrary to the will of God, must be an abomination. I know very well that the ancient Israelites had slaves; but I also know that they practiced bigamy, that brothers married sisters, and that many other things were done which we would not hesitate to brand as sins. . . . Furthermore, slavery was quite different at that time than now. The slaves of the Israelites were white people like themselves, and the children they raised with their female slaves had the same rights as other children, which is clearly evident from the story of Jacob and his twelve sons, who became forefathers of the Twelve Tribes; and of them, four were sons of his wives' slaves. If they had had Americans as fathers, I suppose they would have been sold like other cattle, because it must be very rare, indeed, that an American grants freedom to a child he has sired with a slave.

"People have asked me if I would tolerate having a Negro woman as a daughter-in-law. I must admit that it would not please me very much, but I would rather have it thus than to have grandchildren who are slaves. Of the two evils, I prefer the lesser — in this case, the first alternative which, to be sure, seems unnatural, but still is not associated with sin, whereas the second alternative is equally unnatural and also grossly sinful. They argue that it is not true that all people are descended from Adam and Eve, but that people spring from varied races and have different forefathers. Be that as it may; I can very well grant them the argument even though it has never been proved — it makes absolutely no difference to me. We are, all of us, the children of God, created for the same high destiny, and whereas all of us have our origin in God, all of us are redeemed by the blood of Jesus; all have the same hope of salvation. I believe to the fullest degree that human beings are born with equal rights. Consequently it is repulsive to me to hear people read their Declaration of Independence and deliver bloated Fourth of July orations in honor of liberty while there are millions of slaves among them.

"I am convinced that in time slavery will be abolished either by gentle means or by force, because I believe that institutions founded on injustice cannot survive, but are doomed to fall. I hold that humanity moves slowly but irresistibly forward toward greater perfection. We immigrants, to be sure, can do nothing to abolish slavery; we are too few to accomplish anything for this cause and would merely bring on ourselves hatred and persecution, if we tried. All we can do is to keep ourselves free of the whole slavery system. I am well aware of the argument that when we live in a slave state we may as well own slaves the same as anyone else, but I cannot agree with this. We might as well reason that since we cannot prevent the existence of thieves, robbers, and murderers, we may ourselves become thieves, robbers, and murderers. This is radically wrong; even though we may not be able to prevent others from doing injustice, it is none the less our duty to abstain from anything which our conscience recognizes as unjust. It is, of course, quite a different matter if someone wants to buy slaves in order to grant them their freedom.

"It has so often been maintained that the position of the slaves is just as good as that of the poor wage laborers in Norway that I cannot deny myself the posing of a little comparison. It is true that many of the poorest people in Norway have wretched dwellings, miserable clothes, and at times not even sufficient food for themselves and their families. As a natural consequence they must be permitted to beg, and their need forces them to work for whatever is offered them, which frequently is pitiably little. Not very many, however, live in such beggarly conditions — scarcely any family needs to, if both husband and wife are willing to do their best and if sickness does not strike. Many members of the laboring class even live right well; but let us confine ourselves to the poorest among them. They are free; no one can take their wives away or tear the children from their mothers' arms; no one has the right to mistreat them or sell them; they have good schools for their children, where they are instructed in religion and other useful subjects, and if a certain child is gifted and anxious to learn, he can rise in society to become a great man — yes, even rank next to the king, because all are equal before the law. Anyone who is acquainted with the position of the Negro over here and who honestly considers everything and still is able to say that he would just as soon be a slave in America as a poor laborer in Norway must have quite other feelings and ideas than I."[31]

[31] This quotation indicates that not all the Norwegians in Texas were as strongly

In her letters Mrs. Wærenskjold occasionally refers to Negro maids, hired men, and sharecroppers. She wrote, in 1868, that on the whole the freed Negroes conducted themselves very well; but she also complained that many of them were lazy, cruel to the animals, or so careless with tools that they caused a lot of trouble. In the turmoil of the reconstruction years, she was even moved to wonder — much as she had wished for the freedom of the Negroes — whether it might not have been better for them if their emancipation had been brought about a little more gradually.

Outside of the slavery question, Mrs. Wærenskjold apparently took little interest in American politics. She said nothing about party politics, in the strict sense, in her "Confession of Faith," and a reference in one of her letters indicates that she was repelled by the abusive "bloody shirt" campaigns of the post-Civil War era in the Northern states. In view of her strong democratic feelings, it would have seemed natural for her to sympathize with the aspirations of the Norwegian Liberal party under the leadership of men like Johan Sverdrup and Bjørnstjerne Bjørnson; but if she had such sympathies, she did not express them in any of her extant letters. She read about the fierce political struggles in Norway during the seventies and early eighties, but in faraway Texas the "veto question" and the impeachments of those years evidently seemed much less vital than they did to the people back home in Europe, who were in the midst of the fray. When in 1884 the Liberals achieved a great victory with the introduction of the parliamentary system, Elise confined herself to expressing the hope that there would be less bitterness and hatred in the future. "It has hurt me deeply to think of the recent conditions in my dear fatherland; and I should be most happy if they would improve."

Literature was her greatest intellectual interest. She constantly was writing requests for Norwegian books and attempted, apparently

opposed to slavery as was Mrs. Wærenskjold. In her extant letters she makes no reference to slaveholding among the Norwegians in Four Mile Prairie, but evidently some Norwegians in the larger and more prosperous settlement in Bosque County did own slaves; see Qualey, *Norwegian Settlement*, 207. But even in that area there was no enthusiasm for secession and the Confederacy; William C. Pool, *A History of Bosque County, Texas*, 41 (San Marcos, Texas, 1954). Elise, writing November 18, 1865, stated that "almost all the S—— were opposed to the rebellion." The letters following the "S" are obliterated, but probably the word was "Scandinavians." Tom Spikes, who appeared at the Dickerson trial, seems to have been a former slave who was sheltered by the Wærenskjolds; Derwood Johnson, summary, Texas vs. N. T. Dickerson, p. 13.

without much success, to organize a reading club in the settlement. Her literary tastes were affected by her humanitarianism and by her rather puritanical outlook. Clearly, she believed, not in "art for art's sake" but rather in art for life's sake. Thus, she recommended *Uncle Tom's Cabin* to her sons as a book that properly revealed the nobility of virtue and the loathsomeness of vice. The Norwegian authors who most impressed her were those who championed worthy causes, notably the feminist movement. She spoke highly of several contemporary minor poets, now practically forgotten, such as Elise Sofie Aubert and Ole Kristian Gløersen. Of the latter, she says, "It is remarkable how far he goes in championing the cause of women." Of the "Big Four" in Norwegian literature of that time, she loved Jonas Lie and Alexander Kielland; she regarded Bjørnson coolly, and said that Ibsen "does not appeal to me at all." Not even *A Doll's House,* that gospel of feminism, received an approving word. She did not explain why she disliked Ibsen. Probably, like many of her contemporaries, she found him too "realistic." Since her letters were addressed primarily to people in the homeland, it was natural for her to refer almost exclusively to Norwegian literature; but she did subscribe to American and German papers and periodicals, and she had brought across the Atlantic some French books that she continued to read occasionally.

Another of her interests was immigrant history. Very early she began contributing articles about the Texas settlements to Norwegian publications on both sides of the Atlantic, first to defend these settlements against their detractors, later to tell their story. As the years passed and memories accumulated, her love of the "old days," with their hopes and hardships, deepened. This love and interest, during her old age, brought her into contact with Rasmus B. Anderson, who was engaged in gathering material for a pioneer chronicle of the Norwegians in America. Most of his information about the Texas settlements was obtained directly from Elise Wærenskjold, and his book has been a valuable source for later scholars.

It seems fitting to end our essay about this unusual pioneer woman with a tribute from Anderson's pen:

"Just as I had finished writing the above sketch of this dear old lady, I was startled by the information that she had died January 22,

1895, only two weeks ago. I had recently received a letter from her, in which she tells me that she had returned from a long journey visiting old friends, and that she now had settled down in Hamilton, to remain there until her dying day. She was eighty years old, but a well preserved woman. Mrs. Wærenskjold was an eminent personality. No other Norwegian in Texas was better known than she. She took the deepest interest in all things both in Europe and in America. In her last letter to me, she discussed the death of Svend Foyen [*sic*], which occurred recently in Norway. She was busy writing the history of the Norwegian settlements in Texas. . . . Although I never had the good fortune of meeting Mrs. Wærenskjold, my correspondence with her caused me to esteem most highly this gifted, scholarly, kind, brave and noble woman." [32]

[32] Anderson, *Norwegian Immigration*, 385. Hartvig Johnson, in *Elise Tvede*, 15, mistakenly states that she died November 17, 1895. Svend Foyn died November 28, 1894, at the age of eighty-five; *Salmonsens store illustrerede konversationsleksikon*, 6:995 (Copenhagen, 1897). Mr. N. H. F. Olsen of Dearborn, Michigan, in a letter to the editor, January 5, 1959, states that his father was a flag captain for Svend Foyn. On the day of Foyn's death, at five in the morning, a large kerosene and candle parlor lamp in the Olsen home fell down. "And my Dad said, 'Now died Svend Foyn!' "

PART ONE

In the Beginning

1851–1860

Texas Is the Best State[1]

FOUR MILE PRAIRIE
VAN ZANDT COUNTY, TEXAS
July 9, 1851
MR. T. A. GJESTVANG:

I received your honored letter of May 1 on the first of this month, only two months after you sent it, which is the shortest time I know of for a letter to have covered the distance between Norway and Texas. You enclose in it a copy of several letters from a Frenchman, Captain Tolmer, which appeared in a Norwegian paper, and ask me and other Norwegians here to let you know whether Mr. Tolmer's account is true or false. Even though it seems to me that the contents of the letters should answer this question clearly enough for you and any sensible Norwegian who is not totally ignorant of other countries and especially of the United States (to which Texas has now belonged for several years), I shall comply with your wish as well as time and my meager abilities will permit. I do this partly

[1] This letter, with an introduction by T. Andreas Gjestvang (postmaster at Løiten, Hedmark, Norway) explaining its origin, first appeared in *Hamars budstikke* (Hamar, Norway) and was reprinted in *Morgenbladet* (Christiania), June 17, 18, 1852. A photostat of the *Morgenbladet* reprint in the archives of the Norwegian-American Historical Association forms the basis of the present translation. Under the title, "A Texas Manifesto," this English version appeared in *Norwegian-American Studies and Records*, 20:32–45 (Northfield, 1959). It is a reply to comments made by Captain A. Tolmer, a French traveler of 1849, in a series of ten letters to the French *Journal des Débats* and later published in a book entitled *Scènes de l'Amérique du Nord en 1849* (Leipzig, 1850). A Norwegian translation appeared in *Hamars budstikke* in late 1850 and early 1851. Gjestvang made copies of the letters and sent them to Mrs. Wærenskjold. Wilhelm Wærenskjold wrote to Gjestvang on March 1, 1852, refuting Tolmer's charges. See Blegen, ed., *Land of Their Choice*, 353–368. Gjestvang was vitally interested in America and encouraged a number of families to migrate to Texas.

because of your request and partly to utilize the opportunity to bring my countrymen in Norway some information about this land that could possibly be of some value to those who may plan to come over here.

As you undoubtedly remember, I have been here since 1847, and I have seen a goodly part of this state, since we traveled through Nacogdoches, Cherokee, Henderson, Anderson, Smith, Rusk, and Van Zandt counties, looking for a home which would suit our taste. I stayed for some time in the first three counties mentioned before buying land here in Van Zandt, which I still consider the best of the areas I have seen in Texas. But, without further preliminaries, let us look at Mr. Tolmer's letters.

Your copy begins with the following statement: "I intend in a couple of days to go to Texas, where the struggle between man and nature is even more intense than in the Mississippi Valley." I do not understand what the author means by this expression, since people have far less difficulty in Texas than in Norway — or in any other part of Europe, no doubt — so far as contending with nature is concerned, or in other words in harnessing its forces for the service of man. In Norway, if a person wants to turn a piece of unbroken land into a field, it will cost him much labor; even the cultivated soil must be fertilized if the yield is to be satisfactory — and even so the crop is often destroyed by frost. Here a person merely needs to fence and plow the land and it is ready to be sown. (This is true only of the prairie; the forest land must be cleared of brush and the large trees must be girdled — a belt is cut around the tree, some distance from the ground and a bit deeper than the bark, so as to kill it.)

No one thinks of gathering manure, because it is not needed, and in general the soil is cultivated in a rather slipshod fashion. Thus if a farmer, after having harvested his corn, wants to sow the field to wheat, he does not go to the trouble of clearing away the cornstalks but sows the seed amidst the stalks and all the weeds and then plows it under. That takes care of the matter until harvesttime the following May or June, after which threshing takes just as little work. The wheat is simply placed on the ground and trampled out by horses or oxen, much grain, of course, being lost in the process. Nevertheless, one of our neighbors harvested thirty bushels per acre, having used four bushels for seed. This is above the average, to be sure, but it is equally true that the crops could be much improved by more careful tillage. Rye, barley, and oats are said to give still better yields, but they are raised by very few farmers because the Americans use these grains only as feed for cattle and not for bread. Corn is the most common crop, and corn meal is generally used for baking. It is well liked by those who are used to it, but I must say frankly that I find it to be a poor type of bread.

Cotton is also one of the most important products and is always paid for in cash. Tobacco, flax, and other crops pay well. With the corn, different types of very large and delicious melons, pumpkins, and peas are planted. Potatoes of the Norwegian type are but little raised and are eaten as soon as they grow large enough in the spring (by Eastertime) so I cannot say whether it would pay to produce them, but I should think it would if they were left in the ground until fully grown. Sweet potatoes yield very well if the summer is not exceptionally dry. Among fruits, the peach tree is the only one cultivated; it bears the third year after sprouting. Since grapes, plums, and cherries grow wild, I have no doubt that a person could obtain a fine orchard with little effort if only good trees of various kinds were obtainable. I know from experience that vegetables do very well if one only uses good seed, but, to the best of my knowledge, the seed cannot be either bought or raised here. To be sure, we can get seed from beans, peas, carrots, parsley, radishes, cress, lettuce, fall turnips, etc.; but, on the other hand, I do not believe we can obtain seed here from May turnips, any kind of cabbage or cauliflower, kohlrabi, Swedish turnips, or French turnips (*botfeldtske*), which mature very early and would rot in August when the strong heat comes. It is best to bring along all sorts of seed. And all these things can be raised without manure and with only the most perfunctory type of tillage.

From what I have said, people can gather how much of a struggle it is to wrest from nature the daily bread; the struggle with the wild animals of the forest is of about the same severity. To be sure, quite a few beasts of prey are found here, for there are panthers (a kind of tiger, the size of a dog but shaped like a cat), bears, wolves, foxes, opossums, skunks, several types of snakes, and alligators in the lakes and rivers. But there is enough food for all these animals so they do not need to attack human beings. It is customary, therefore, when out traveling, especially with a wagon, to sleep in the open either in the wagon or on the ground. A person can sleep quite securely, even though unarmed and far from people, whether it be on the prairie or in the woods. I might mention that old man Engelhoug lives all by himself in a little cabin he built in a lowland near a lake where there are alligators (my husband shot one of them), but he spends his time there quite undisturbed, even though it is in exactly such lowlands that wild animals are found. On my travels I myself usually sleep out, and, except at first when I did not know the country, I have felt no more fear out in the woods or on the prairie, though at times a couple of days' journey from people, than I did at home in Norway behind well-locked doors.

All the time I have been in Texas I have not heard of a single case in which human beings were attacked or harmed by wild animals. At times, however, they will resist if molested. I have heard of people — I believe there were two — who were bitten by snakes, but they recovered without difficulty. But snakes can be a nuisance and may crawl clear up to the second story, especially a type called the chicken snake because it eats chickens and eggs, which it swallows whole. The reason for its intrusion into houses is that the hens usually have their nests under the beds and up in the lofts. These snakes are harmless, however; but, of course, such an uninvited guest can put a scare into newcomers, as happened to the Grøgaards and me in Nacogdoches, where such a snake had made its way to the loft.

It is a peculiar thing that most of the animals here are more amiable than those in Norway. I have not seen a single mad bull here, while most of those I saw in Norway were very fierce. Neither is the danger for the domestic animals by far as great as one might expect, despite the fact that cattle, horses, and pigs run about in the woods without any supervision and at times may be away for days or even weeks and months, especially during the winter when the wild animals are the most dangerous. I have never heard of a cow or a horse being killed or wounded by a wild animal, but I suppose it may happen, though very seldom, that a little calf or a young colt may be if it is not kept at home. It is seldom, also, that a grown hog is killed, but many young pigs are lost during the winter if they are not kept in during the first weeks. Sheep also are in danger if they are not penned at night. I believe what I have said will prove that the struggle between man and nature is not particularly fierce nor hazardous.

Next Mr. Tolmer talks about the poisoned arrows of the Comanche Indians, and the Texans' rifles. I cannot say anything about the first-mentioned articles because as yet I have not seen a single Indian; so far as the Texans are concerned, a person has nothing to fear from them unless he gets into trouble with them — then they really are much too prone to avenge every real or fancied insult with a bullet or a stab. But I am certain there is no land in the world where a person has less reason to fear assault or robbery than here, where such things are unheard of. So when Tolmer says it is a miracle that he is still alive after having been in Texas a couple of weeks, one can only laugh. His whole silly story did indeed give me, and several others who happened to be here, a hearty laugh when I received the letter and read it to them.

It is true that the population of Texas is mixed; it is mixed as is the population of the other states in the Union, but to no greater degree. The inhabitants consist primarily of migrants from the other states, and they are no worse or more immoral than in the older areas; they have their vices and virtues as in all other countries. They are, as already remarked, very quick to avenge themselves, and in all business dealings with them one must guard against being "taken by the nose" because they look upon cheating about as people in Norway regarded smuggling during my childhood. Otherwise they are very friendly and helpful, not only toward their own people but also toward foreigners. As proof of this I will merely mention that a Norwegian widow who lives in Nacogdoches (the same town pictured, in such dark colors, by Tolmer) with a large family of children not only received substantial gifts in the form of food and clothing, but, besides, the tuition fees for her children — which are quite high here — were paid for her. This was done by people, some of whom had never seen her. Consequently we do not need any public poor relief here, and you will look in vain for a beggar, because anyone who wants to work can earn a living, and those who really are in need will receive ample help without begging for it.

Furthermore, one cannot praise too highly that real freedom and equality which exist here and make themselves felt in numerous ways, not only in social relationships, where the poor are treated with the same politeness as the rich, the laborer like the official, but also in public matters. Every adult male has the right to vote irrespective of his economic status, and similarly all are obliged to defend their country no matter what their social position may be. All other duties as well as privileges are shared alike by everyone. It is not here as in Norway, where equality and liberty are found on paper but not in real life.

This equality is a natural consequence of economic conditions and of the system of government. When everybody can earn enough for an independent living, the poor will not cringe before the rich nor the latter treat the former with arrogance. Similarly, when public officials are chosen by the people, and only for a certain number of years, they will not be tempted to be overbearing. But it cannot be denied that this method of choosing civil servants has its drawbacks, because many ignorant people are put into positions which they are not qualified to fill. I mentioned above that Americans are inclined to cheat. From this a person might conclude that they also would be given to stealing, but this is so far from being the case that I am sure there are few countries where one's possessions are as safe as they are here. Thievery is absolutely despised and is hardly ever practiced, except on rare occasions by Negroes. Therefore locks are seldom found on houses, frequently not even doors. Nevertheless, a person can leave his house both days and nights, yes, even weeks, without missing anything when he returns. Even in the towns you can leave stuff out on the sidewalks without losing anything, an experience we ourselves had in Nacogdoches. And these are the people whom Captain Tolmer accuses of having besmirched themselves with all sorts of vices. What a disgraceful lie! Besides Americans, we have here immigrants from Germany, England, France, Denmark, and Norway; that these people are not worse than other human beings I hope will be believed without further assurances.

There are very few free Negroes here, but, unfortunately, there are many slaves because most rich Americans are slaveowners. Much as I despise slavery, I cannot deny that the slaves here are treated rather well and that numbers of them are better off in many respects than the free laborers in Europe. But the loss of liberty cannot be replaced by anything. Since there are no Indians in the part of Texas where I have been, I can say nothing about them.

When Tolmer says that the Americans are mixed, some with Indians, some with runaway slaves, he lies, because they are entirely too proud for that. But it is difficult to find a single assertion which is not a lie. It is hard for me to think it ever occurred to him that people would accept this product of his at face value; it strikes me as nothing but a poorly written adventure story. I wonder if the people in Norway were not simply confused if they took Tolmer's account as anything but a piece of fiction. It is impossible for me to believe that Tolmer would have the audacity to offer as truth such a mass of gross, and in part palpable, lies to so highly cultured a nation as the French.

His ignorance of geography is so obvious that I believe any schoolboy would notice it. If he means to say that he rode horseback from New Orleans to Galveston, then he must never have been there, because this trip can only be taken by sea. Furthermore, there is no lack of fine horses, and it would not be difficult to steal them, as they roam about to suit their own fancy. But, as already stated, you do not need to fear robbery and thieving in this country.

Neither will any American allow himself to be threatened with a whip; the good Mr. Tolmer would soon have had a bullet through his body if he had dared such a thing. To say that everybody here is a judge or a general is, of course, a ridiculous overstatement, but undoubtedly there are quite a few who fought as generals against Mexico during the war of liberation, when the Texans gained great fame for heroism. Similarly, since officials are elected for a set number of years, it follows that there must be many who have served as judges or in other capacities.

Tolmer's statement that Galveston is the capital of Texas reveals an inexcusable ignorance, since Austin, as everyone knows, is the capital city. His travel route from Galveston to Wisconsin also proves that, far from being well acquainted with this country, he did not even have a map of Texas.[2] . . . But if the good Tolmer has neglected to study the geography of the country, he has devoted himself with so much the greater diligence to the language, since he even understood the "thief" language, which he says the judges and the generals made use of. From what I have already written, it will be easily understood that it is not customary here to travel with an escort of either Americans or Indians; only the most miserable coward could think of doing such a thing. That he sat down at an unpainted wooden table is quite believable but not that it was dirty, because the cleanliness of the Americans is very well known.

I cannot say anything about the previous inhabitants of Nacogdoches; I wonder how Tolmer had become so well acquainted with them and with the former appearance of the town. Had he already been there on some earlier occasion? Now the town is inhabited by Americans, a few Germans, and a still smaller number of Norwegians and Frenchmen. Most of them are well-to-do people engaged in trade. In the surrounding area are found a few Mexicans, who are usually held in slight esteem, whether justly or unjustly I cannot say. That there is as little cause to fear assault and robbery in Nacogdoches as in other parts of Texas should be obvious from what I have already said. There is no hotel there called "The Red Eagle" and no Spanish hotelkeeper; there are only two hotels, both owned by Americans. The town is too insignificant to have gates or portals; there is no river there spanned by a bridge — only a little creek crossed by a log. No boats can be used in it because it is so narrow that a person can usually jump across it. Neither are there any prairies in the neighborhood, and still less crocodiles and jaguars. (These animals are not found in Texas but, as already stated, the related panther and alligator are.) Nor are the Americans afraid of beasts of prey — no more than they would be afraid of giving the good Captain Tolmer a sound beating for all his lies if he were here. Undoubtedly there are quite a few wild horses in Texas and they can be tamed, but I do not suppose anyone is simple enough to believe that a person can, without further ado, jump astride a wild horse and ride it. Dogs

---

[2] Here follows a brief exposition of Tolmer's ignorance of Texas geography, but without access to his account, the analysis is obscure and has been omitted here.

are not used for hunting human beings. Tolmer undoubtedly had in mind the brutality of the Spaniards when they conquered America.

Such a house as the one Tolmer describes, with iron doors, etc., is not found in the vicinity of Nacogdoches, likely not in all Texas; the whole incident is nothing but fiction from beginning to end, since nothing even remotely like it has happened in the vicinity of Nacogdoches, and the people whom he mentions by name are absolutely nonexistent.

I notice that I have forgotten one of Mr. Tolmer's charges, namely, that a person must not count on justice in our courts. No doubt this is in part true, but to no greater degree than in old Norway. The laws there, as here, have their flaws and often are not put in as clear and definite language as they ought to be. This may cause them to be misunderstood or even on occasion to be interpreted in accordance with the individual opinions and wishes of the jurymen. I must say that in some respects the laws here strike me as superior to those in Norway, aiming especially at protecting women and children against want. Thus, while an unmarried man must pay a tax on all his possessions, a man with a family may own $250 worth of property tax exempt. Similarly, if an unmarried man is in debt, the creditor can seize all his property as security, while a married man can hold the following free of distraint: a family homestead (but not above 200 acres of land or, in cities, property in excess of $2,000), all furniture and kitchen utensils (not above $200 in value), all farm implements (not above $50 in value), all implements and books in the case of craftsmen or professional men, five milk cows, one pair of oxen or one horse, twenty pigs, and provisions for one year. Neither can the creditors seize anything which the wife has added to the estate, either through marriage or later, if she has registered it with the authorities as her property. The purpose of these laws is, of course, to protect women and children against want. I might mention that every male person between the ages of twenty-one and forty-five is required to pay a head tax which varies from $.75 to $1.50, and $.20 on every $100 he owns. These are the only taxes I know of in Texas.

You are acquainted with my views about immigration to this country. I believe now, as formerly, that there are many thousands in

Norway who would be far happier over here, namely, the growing class of laborers and cotters — yes, also the less well-to-do farmers and handicraftsmen; in short, all people in Norway who live in economic dependence and have to work for others. Since the wages here are so much better, people like that could work themselves up in a short time to an independent position free of worries about the daily bread. On the other hand, anyone who is well situated in Norway ought, in my opinion, to remain. Provided he can lead an independent life there and has the means to hire others to work for him, he will not be better off here but probably worse, since he might not be able to hire help (a man is not paid less than $10 a month) and thus would be forced to do much heavy work that is quite unpleasant for those who are not used to it. Likewise — at least to begin with — he would have to do without many of the conveniences and pleasures of life that the more well-to-do people in Norway are accustomed to. For the poor and destitute, on the other hand, who have never enjoyed things like these, but from early childhood have been inured to drudgery and toil, there is little to lose and much to gain. In general, it depends much on a person's character and ability to work whether he will be satisfied or dissatisfied. Land can still be obtained in our neighborhood for $.35 to $2 per acre. Lots as small as 320 acres are still obtainable at $.50 per acre, but this will not last long, as land is rising in price.

I have already spoken about the various field crops. All kinds of domesticated animals also thrive well and can be raised to good advantage, but a person must give them some attention if they are to produce a proper income. For instance, a person ought to provide himself with hay during the summer. This does not require any tillage, because an overabundance of good hay grows wild; one only needs to cut and stack it to have butter and milk all winter. Most people, however, prefer to do without milk and butter throughout the winter and let the cattle shift for themselves during this season. The same is true with pigs; if one lets them run about in meadows and woods with their young while these are quite small, the increase will be very slow because most of the little ones will be killed. The sows should be kept in for several weeks after farrowing. Sheep are very profitable, but they must be locked in every night to keep them from being killed by the wolves. All types of poultry, as well as bees, do well. There are still a great many deer about, so the hunter is richly rewarded. He will also find numerous smaller animals like rabbits and squirrels (which are very tasty) as well as many wild birds such as turkeys, geese, various types of ducks, prairie chickens, and, in the fall, countless swarms of doves, besides smaller birds. The doves come by the millions; they look like a dark cloud and there is a sound in the sky as if a great storm is approaching. My husband killed about thirty with one shot, and where they roost at night whole wagonloads can be killed. But they are not this numerous every year. There are not as many wild berries here as in Norway nor as many varieties. Grapevines, however, grow in profusion everywhere, and another wild fruit, the persimmon, is also very delicious. Wild honey in great plenty can be gathered by those who know how.

A family with children will get ahead much easier than one without, since labor is of greater value here than in Norway and many kinds of work can be done by children just as well as by adults. The main argument which can be advanced against immigration is that of health, because a person must be prepared to come down with ague, something very few newcomers escape entirely, though they undoubtedly must thank their own carelessness and cocksureness for it. It is not a mortal disease, however, and on the whole is not very serious for those who have the proper medicine and take proper care. In New Orleans immigrants should provide themselves with quinine, castor oil, and other useful medicines. But they should be especially careful in the taking of calomel, improper use of which undoubtedly has caused the death of several Norwegians.

I believe Texas is the best of the states to migrate to, partly because the climate is milder and more pleasant than in the Northern states and partly because the land is cheaper. Furthermore, without owning land a person can here acquire as many cattle as he pleases, and, finally, a person can sustain himself with so much less effort, since less is required for housebuilding, for getting food for the animals, etc., etc., than in colder climates.

I will now conclude, despite the fact that I could say much more about Texas. But time is short and conditions very difficult for me, as I am constantly interrupted. So I must ask your pardon for sending you such a piece of hasty work as this.[3]

Respectfully,

E. WÆRENSKJOLD

An Odd Form of Worship [4]

FOUR MILE PRAIRIE

July 25, 1852

MR. T. A. GJESTVANG:

I have had the pleasure of receiving the letter you were kind enough to send me enclosed in the one to Grimseth, and I sent both of them immediately to old Nordboe by Cleng Peerson.[5] But the six letters you mentioned have not yet arrived. From your letter I understand that a large group of people intend to emigrate this year. I do wish all of them would comprehend most thoroughly at least one thing, namely this: that the one who neither knows how nor wants to work, and who does not possess a sufficient amount of money, will

[3] Twenty-three other settlers in Texas signed brief statements condemning Tolmer's account as "the most miserable product that can be bred by mendacity and ignorance," to quote one of them. Among the signatories was John (Johannes) Nordboe, probably the first Norwegian settler in Texas, who declared that Mrs. Wærenskjold's letter was correct in every detail, while the accounts that the "arch-liar Tolmer has strewn broadcast" were "unadulterated lies." The well-known Cleng Peerson confirmed this judgment. Cleng Peerson (1782–1865), father of Norwegian migration to America, was an almost legendary figure who journeyed on foot from settlement to settlement. He had a special fondness for Texas and advocated colonization in that state. He died there and was buried at Norse. See Blegen, *Norwegian Migration, 1825–1860,* 185, 192–194, 382–385.

[4] This letter appeared in *Arbeider-foreningernes blad* (Christiania), January 1, 1853. With minor editorial changes, it is given here as translated and edited, with several other "Texas letters," by Lyder Unstad in *Norwegian-American Studies and Records,* 8:39–57 (Northfield, 1934). A file of *Arbeider-foreningernes blad* is in the library of the University of Oslo. A photostatic copy of the letter was furnished by Professor Kenneth O. Bjork.

[5] For information about Nordboe and references to pertinent literature, see Arne Odd Johnsen, "Johannes Nordboe and Norwegian Immigration," in *Norwegian-American Studies and Records,* 8:23–38. According to this article, Nordboe died "during the sixties" in Tarrant County, Texas. In a letter to the editor, Derwood Johnson states that Nordboe's will was probated December 11, 1856, and that "he must have died prior to the admission of his will to probate." Mr. Johnson continues, "A possible explanation of this contradiction may be in the fact that John P. [Nordboe] had a son named John who may have moved to Tarrant County." (November 26, 1958.)

not be successful in America. For, since workers' wages are high, one can easily understand that it does not pay to hire people to do everything. I cannot impress this too strongly upon the minds of my countrymen; those coming over here with other expectations must necessarily be disappointed. Thus there is a person among us who every day pours forth his abuse of America but who has not since he arrived in this country worked enough to pay his board for a single day. He is, to be sure, an exception; but there are altogether too many who have not as yet grasped the meaning of the American saying, "Time is money."

Bjerke left us at once and went to Rusk, but he has left there also, with his wife and mother-in-law. I presume that most of your acquaintances write to you and no doubt they can tell you much better than I how they are faring.

August 4

On the day after I had begun writing this letter, I received the package containing the six letters. Much therein was for me.

This summer we have a good crop of all kinds of farm produce, so the expected immigrants will find the prices of foodstuffs considerably lower than during the last two years.

I have nothing of interest to tell you at present, since in my last letter I told you about conditions in this country. Well, yes, I must tell you a little about camp meetings, which are the oddest form of Christian worship that any person can imagine. Somewhere in the woods they build a shed — that is to say, a roof that rests on posts but has neither walls nor floor; there are a few logs to sit on, as well as a raised platform that serves as pulpit. Five preachers were present [when I was there]; at times there are even more, and they continue preaching day and night for eight days. The people in the vicinity gather around the camp, some in wagons and tents and others in small log houses that they have built. All of them bring from home sufficient food and household utensils for the time they expect to stay. We arrived at the camp at noon and left the place at midnight. We were at once invited for dinner by two American families, after which we entered the church, where nothing out of the ordinary took place at the time. But later on in the evening the womenfolk wandered out into the forest for the so-called secret prayers; the menfolk went in another direction for the same purpose. They alternately sang psalms and poured forth long prayers, which they took turns reciting. They become so inspired on these occasions that one after another they begin to sing and clap their hands, crying out "Glory! Glory!" as loudly as they can. They begin pounding on the ones nearest to them, throwing themselves on their knees or on their backs, laughing and crying — in short, conducting themselves like perfectly insane people. At the evening service the same comic performance took place, and the preachers exerted themselves to the utmost to rouse the people to the highest state of ecstasy. At these camp meetings people are baptized, married, and tendered the Lord's Supper. The emotions that the whole thing aroused were hardly devotional.[6]

Please accept for yourself and the whole family the most friendly and cordial greetings from Wilhelm, Otto, and myself.

ELISE WÆRENSKJOLD

A Little Town Is Springing Up [7]

FOUR MILE PRAIRIE
Third Day of Christmas, 1852

To MRS. THOMINE DANNEVIG:

A few days after Otto was born, he got a little colt which will thus be two years old in the spring and will then be broken in. It is already so gentle that Wilhelm can sit on it whenever he wishes, so I think it will be a good riding horse by the time Otto gets big enough to ride.

[6] In the original the sentence reads, "De følelser, det hele opvakte, vare intet mindre end andægtige." A literal translation of the last part of the sentence would be, "were nothing less than devotional," but this plainly gives a wrong meaning to the phrase.

[7] Letters in this volume addressed to Mrs. Thomine Dannevig and to her family were published, with an introduction by Emil Olsen, in *Tønsbergs blad* (Tønsberg, Norway), May 11–26, 1925. Olsen received the letters from the Dannevig family. A scrapbook of the clippings is in the archives of the Norwegian-American Historical Association; it includes a letter of September 29, 1868, to Mrs. Kaja Poppe, and one of December 20, 1887, to Madam Basberg, which will follow in the present volume. Mrs. Lars Tellefsen (Thomine) Dannevig had been Elise's best friend in Lillesand, and Elise was godmother to Thomine's older son, Thorvald, to whom several of these letters are addressed. (Elise's youngest son was named Thorvald.) Information furnished in an interview with Miss Vally Dannevig of Oslo, daughter of Nils, who was Thomine's younger son; Ingrid Gaustad Semmingsen to the editor, May 19, 1959.

It is named after my father's brown horse, Perris, which you perhaps remember; we have another beautiful colt named Alida.

I think your boys would enjoy seeing all of our many domestic animals. Otto already has a lot of fun with them, especially with the poultry, of which I have various kinds: hens, turkeys, guinea hens, geese, and two kinds of ducks. When I give them grain, and they all gather around me, it is Otto's greatest pleasure to run among them with a little stick, and he is terribly pleased when they scamper. He also wanted to chase after the pigs when they were small, but I didn't dare leave him alone with them for fear the sows would bite him.

My wishes for my little Otto's future are very modest. All I ask is that he may become an upright and able farmer, possessed of such knowledge as every cultured man should have. I have always had a liking for farm and country life, and if one is otherwise happy in his position, I cannot imagine a more pleasant or more independent state, for in this country a tiller of the soil is respected as much as anyone else, be he official or merchant. This is not as in Norway, where the farmers constitute a lower class.

I would like to have various kinds of fruit pits and seeds sent over here to be planted. We have many good things in Norway that are lacking here; but it is not the fault of the land, for we could hardly expect to harvest what we have never sown. I haven't been able to get a simple thing like ale until recently because of the lack of yeast; but as the last immigrants brought yeast with them, almost all of us brewed ale for Christmas, and it has never tasted so good to me as now. I haven't tasted a glass of wine in four years. If I could get fruit, I would certainly have wine and juice too. A person certainly misses refreshing drinks when he is athirst from fever, especially as cold water is looked upon as harmful.

I suppose I should try to tell you a little about myself and the few acquaintances you have here, all of whom, as far as I know, are doing fine. [Erick] Bache, Andreas Ørbeck, and Christian Reiersen and his wife [*Ouline Ørbeck*] visited us at Christmas; all seemed to be well content. For newcomers to this place, the Baches have been extremely lucky, as they have been entirely spared by the fever. I haven't visited them yet, and it will no doubt be a long time before that happens, because I cannot ride such a distance with Otto, and my husband has got it into his head that he doesn't want to ride in an oxcart. They say that Andreas [Ørbeck] will marry Gina Reiersen one of these days. Old [Ole] Reiersen has passed away. Andreas is apparently earning good money; he is well paid for managing Vinzent's store in Rusk and, besides, has a flourishing business here, which is handled by one Olsen, from Hedmark. He rents the store from J. R. Reiersen, around whose place a little town is springing up. A man named Grimseth from Hedmark has built a house next to the store where he expects to sell liquor, and a widow, also from Hedmark, plans to set up a bakery and restaurant. Olsen is putting up a mill and a cotton ginning machine and is also going to build a house. A smith from Hedmark who works for Olsen is also going to build, as his wife and children are expected, and Reiersen himself will put up a schoolhouse. Few of our little towns could boast of so many houses at the start. Reiersen is doing fine, as he has several steady roomers who pay pretty well.

As for my own insignificant person, I have generally been well, but last summer I had the misfortune to break my left arm. It didn't pain me much, but my hand became crooked and has not yet quite regained its strength.

Last summer there was quite an unusual amount of sickness here. We were spared for a long time, but then Wilhelm caught the fever, and since there was no quinine in the store or anywhere in the neighborhood, he couldn't break it. Anne, the maid, had to do part of his work, so she took sick too, and when I was left alone, Otto and I also got it. After a few days, however, we were lucky enough to get some quinine. It is wonderful how quickly and surely one can break the fever with this medicine. The shops quickly sold out to the doctors, so the Norwegians got little. The result was that nine people died, most of whom could surely have been saved if they had had this remedy. A widow who lives in our old house had fever every day for several weeks and at last grew so feeble that we feared for her life; but finally she got hold of some quinine, and from the moment she took it, she was entirely cured.

My husband had sent out an invitation to people to pledge an annual contribution for a Norwegian Lutheran pastor, and in half a day something over $70 was pledged by only half of the settlers; it seemed likely that the matter would progress satisfactorily, but these many deaths have so depressed most of the people that the project has for the time being come to a complete standstill. We are now expecting Gjestvang and ten or eleven families from Hedmark. If they should settle down here, it is possible that something may yet come of it.

There are all kinds of religions here, as you no doubt know, but most people are Methodists. They hold various kinds of services; of these, their camp meetings deserve mention. They are held preferably in the fall and last for several days, during which several ministers preach day and night, baptize adults as well as children, perform marriages, and administer Holy Communion. People assemble from miles around; some live in wagons, some in tents, and some in lodginghouses that have been erected near the place where the camp meetings are held. There is no church there, but an open shed serves as one; into it some benches are brought which are perfectly in keeping with the building. People bring food with them in abundance and are most hospitable.

There is nothing unusual about their sermons or hymns, or their baptism or the sacrament of the Lord's Supper, which are all administered about as with us; but in the afternoon all the men go to one place and all the women to another for private prayer. There they alternate song and prayer, which one of them says in a very loud voice. During these long and vehement prayers, they kneel at first, each in his own place, but little by little, as they become more excited, soon one and then another will begin to scream and cry out, clap his hands, slap those standing nearest, throw himself down on the ground, and on the whole act like a madman or one possessed by the devil. The others press around the ecstatic ones and continue singing and praying. The same mad scene takes place in the evening after the sermon and after the minister's most zealous incitement. Apparently they believe that they cannot get into Heaven unless they take it by storm. There was no edification for me in this. Several of the Norwegians have abandoned their Lutheran faith. Andreas [Ørbeck] and Mads Vinzent were baptized and went over to the Campbellites, Marie Grøgaard to the Episcopalians, Mother

Staack to the Methodists, and her brother to the Baptists.[8] I wish very much that we could soon get a good Lutheran pastor.

The Fourth of July was celebrated by the Norwegians in the settlement, one and all, each person contributing either food or money. Wærenskjold gave half an ox and $.50. They gathered in the morning and continued celebrating a good twenty-four hours. They ate and drank lustily. A few danced a little. Wærenskjold made a speech. As for me, I would rather have had nothing to do with the entire party, but such things are just to Wilhelm's liking, especially when he can be at the head of the whole affair. Of what we usually call amusements, I have few or none. My greatest joy is Otto, and I also have a great satisfaction in seeing our various domestic animals thrive and multiply.

Now you must soon send me a letter again. To get letters from Norway is one of my greatest pleasures, but, with the exception of Gjestvang, almost no one writes except when immigrants come; then we usually get a lot of newspapers, too, and a few books, which we read over and over until the next year, when immigrants come again.

[ELISE WÆRENSKJOLD]

A Temperance Society

FOUR MILE PRAIRIE
January 6, 1857

[To MRS. THOMINE DANNEVIG:]

It was a great as well as unexpected joy, after such a long period of time, to receive the large package of letters from you, for which I thank you sincerely.

You must not think that I have really given up hope of seeing

---

[8] In *Tønsbergs blad* the word used is *Carmelitterne* (the Carmelites), but it should undoubtedly be "Campbellites." Campbellite is the colloquial name of a religious sect founded in Virginia by the Reverend Alexander Campbell (1788–1866). "Mother" Staack was the wife of James Hendrick Staack, a native of Lauenburg, Germany, who settled in Texas in 1846. Born Ingeborg Hansen, she was first married to Jens Jenson. Her brother was Knud Hansen.

you again, but for some years yet we cannot afford to go, and besides the children are still too small to get much benefit or pleasure out of such a trip.[9] If all goes well for the next seven or eight years, however, it could happen that we might be able to visit our beloved native land.

No doubt you know that cattle raising is our principal means of livelihood. We do not plan to sell the cows, just the steers, until we can acquire about two hundred calves a year. This spring we can expect about seventy. Cows and calves are now $15 each, and a three-year-old unbroken ox costs about the same. When it is trained for work, it costs much more. We have four mares, a horse, and a mule. The latter is unusually gentle and sure-footed. It is the children's and my riding horse. Niels sits in my lap and Otto behind me. We do have a four-wheeled carriage but very seldom use it.

We have sixty-two sheep, and this month and next we are expecting many lambs. I help clip the sheep, but I am not very good at it. I can do only one while the others clip two, whereas Wilhelm can keep up with anyone. He is very quick at all kinds of work. I do not know how many pigs we have, not because we have so many but because pigs are so difficult to keep track of.

Because I hate liquor, it is a great joy to me that Wilhelm never tastes it. He organized a temperance society in our settlement, and since then the community has become so respectable and sober that it is a real pleasure. All of us Norwegians, about eighty persons counting young and old, can come together for a social gathering without having strong drink, but we do have coffee, ale, milk, and mead at our gatherings, and food in abundance. In the older Norwegian settlement [Brownsboro] there is a disgusting amount of drinking, among both Norwegians and Americans. A Norwegian boy shot himself as a result of his addiction to drink, and recently an American was stabbed to death by another American, likewise because of drunkenness. Drinking, quarreling, and fighting are common here. Yes, liquor destroys both body and soul.

You are really going to get a short letter in answer to your long one, but this is the twelfth letter I have written in a week, and I

[9] Elise's second son, Niels, was born in 1853.

have three more to write by noon tomorrow — and you can well imagine how little time I have for correspondence.

[ELISE WÆRENSKJOLD]

We Have Organized a Reading Club [10]

[FOUR MILE PRAIRIE
AUTUMN, 1857]

[TO THE EDITOR:]

Even though we Norwegians find ourselves content and happy in our new home, which is thousands of miles away from our mother country, we still cherish in our hearts the memory of old Norway and our countrymen over there. Every possible link with the beloved land of our birth is important and precious to us. For that reason, the Norwegian, Swedish, and Danish immigrants of this little settlement of Four Mile Prairie have organized a reading club. As the group comprises only sixteen families, the total fund for the purchase of books is very small ($22). We are presuming, therefore, to ask our countrymen who may be interested in their distant brothers and sisters in Texas for a gift of some books, which may be delivered to the publisher, Jacob Dybwad, of Christiania. We should appreciate it if the kind donors would write their names in the book or books that they are good enough to give. We shall gratefully welcome every book, new or old. Because I am personally acquainted with several of the publishers, I am taking the liberty of appealing to them for small donations. They must have many works that will not be sold out. Many good books of the older authors have perhaps little or no value in Norway, as they have been supplanted by the more recent writers. That is not the case here, where we so rarely have the opportunity to procure Norwegian books, since very few had the forethought to bring books with them when they left Norway. The various editors would do us a great service if they would reprint these lines in their respective newspapers.

For those who may be interested, I shall add that there are three

[10] This letter appeared in *Morgenbladet*, February 26, 1858. A typescript is in the archives of the Norwegian-American Historical Association.

Norwegian settlements here, with approximately three hundred inhabitants, including eight Danes and one Swede. The oldest settlement [Normandy], begun in 1845, is about as large as this one and the newest one combined. Most of the people were poor when they came, but all of them have prospered more or less. Families can be found who were in debt when they arrived but are now well off. Texas, on the whole, is a remarkably good place for the poor, as they can always get work with good pay and soon become independent. This is all the more true, because government land is cheap — half a dollar an acre. All white men are treated with equal courtesy. For those back home who have been accustomed to servants, life here would perhaps be less pleasant, since help is difficult to obtain and very expensive.

In 1854 a theological candidate, A. E. Fridrichsen, was called as pastor to Four Mile Prairie.[11] That same year, a small, simple church was begun in the settlement and was dedicated immediately after the pastor's arrival the following year. Each member paid from $3 to $8 yearly toward his salary, not including the festal offerings and fees for baptisms, funerals, and the like. Some widows and spinsters subscribed $1 or $2. It would be fine if we could get a Christian-minded minister, for Pastor Fridrichsen plans to return home this winter. But he definitely must not come expecting any temporal gain, because he cannot count on more than $300 annually and a simple house, from all three settlements.

In closing, I pray that all my friends and acquaintances in Norway will accept affectionate greetings from

ELISE WÆRENSKJOLD

(nee Tvede)

[11] Anders Emil Fridrichsen, one of the most enigmatic and picturesque individuals to appear in the Norwegian-American Lutheran Church, has become a somewhat controversial figure. He migrated to Texas in 1854 and served there until 1857, when he went to southern Minnesota. During his long career as a minister, he got into numerous feuds with more conventional men of the cloth. See Kenneth O. Bjork, *West of the Great Divide: Norwegian Migration to the Pacific Coast, 1847–1893,* 303–319 (Northfield, 1958).

Neighbors Here Are Very Kind

FOUR MILE PRAIRIE
October 16, 1858

[To MRS. THOMINE DANNEVIG:]

You probably heard from your brother, to whom I have written a couple of times this summer, that I again expected a little boy, and now I can tell you, God be praised, that the little baby arrived happy and well on the fourth of this month. I cannot tell you how glad I was that everything went well because, after all, I am no longer young, and I was worried for fear I might have to leave my beloved children. Neither Wilhelm nor I have a single relative in this country, so it isn't easy to say what he would have done with the children if I had died. It is absolutely against the custom of this country for a white girl to keep house for a widower — and as for a stepmother, well, they are seldom good.

But, thank God, I am entirely well again and hope that the Almighty will grant me yet a few years with my sweet little boys. The little one shall be named Thorvald August after your dear Thorvald and a little German friend I had on the emigrant ship. I can truly say that the neighbors here are very kind to each other on occasions such as this, for they look after one another and provide food. That is to say, our neighbors in the country; the city women, on the other hand, follow the American customs.

I wrote to Hansen a few months ago about a minister who would like to come here. I cannot tell you how much I wish we might again get someone who could instill a love and respect for the Christian teachings in the young people.

Your acquaintances here are well. As you must know, [Erick] Bache has, besides the store, also a hotel. Recently a company of circus riders and similar performers were here in Prairieville, and Mother Bache made a lot of money. Among the attractions was a living skeleton, a mulatto who, with the exception of his head and neck, was nothing but skin and bones. They said it was a frightful sight to behold, but I would have liked very much to see him because probably nowhere on this earth could his like be found. Wilhelm and the little boys saw the entire show.

For the last two or three months we have had a teacher [*Sigurd Ørbeck*] for our little boys. He gets his food and lodging for his work. He also instructs some of the neighbors' children.

[ELISE WÆRENSKJOLD]

A Visit from Elling Eielsen [12]

FOUR MILE PRAIRIE
March 24, 1860

MY DEAR FRIENDS:

Since a Norwegian who has been in Texas seven years is going back to Norway, I will send you these lines. Because there are so many I want to write to, I hope you will excuse my writing in such a way that the letter may be passed around to all my friends in Lillesand.

My husband and children, as well as I myself, are getting along well and are in good health, as usual. Last year Otto and Niels went to the school taught by Sigurd Ørbeck, who stayed at our house, but now Ørbeck is bookkeeper at the sawmill in Brownsboro. The first of April the little boys will start going to the English school in Prairieville, which is two and a half English miles from us. Every Sunday they go to Sunday school to learn Bible history and the catechism.

This winter we had a visit from a minister, Elling Eielsen, who was ordained in Wisconsin, where he and his family live. He is a Haugean, to be sure, but a particularly capable person who is an untiring worker even though he is an old man. He visited all the Norwegians and preached every day — and nearly all day. Thus, the day we had Communion, he preached an especially good sermon first, then gave a long talk to the communicants. In the afternoon he first talked with the people about instituting religious instruction and managed to arrange for us to have a Sunday school. Following that, he took up the temperance question, in which he is keenly interested.[13]

[12] "My dear friends" were undoubtedly the Dannevig family; this letter, which was published in *Tønsbergs blad*, May 16, 1925, appeared with the Dannevig collection mentioned *ante*, n. 7.

[13] Elling Eielsen (1804–83), famous Norwegian pioneer pastor, emigrated to the

He spent most of his time in the Norwegian settlement at Browns-boro, where the Norwegians are great lovers of intoxicating drinks. He and my husband have organized a new temperance society there, as the one that my husband started five years ago died out almost immediately, partly because they completely misunderstood the rules and thought that one might drink hard liquor if only one did not become intoxicated, and partly because there was no one who took charge of promoting the cause. This time we hope that with God's help it may fare better, since they seemed to be deeply moved by the pastor's presentation and admonitions.

He confirmed four adults who had not wanted to be confirmed when Fridrichsen was the pastor here. One of these was a married woman.

Eielsen undertook this long and difficult journey without arrang-ing a guarantee of compensation for his expenses and his time — in fact, without the slightest indication that he expected any pay whatsoever. He does not accept offerings. Of course they paid him something, but I very much doubt that his expenses were covered. I presume that he received about $100 in the three settlements. It was the general wish that he would move down here to be our pastor, and I do not think we could find anyone better fitted for the work here.

[Johan] Reinert Reiersen has moved to Brownsboro, where he, my husband, and Ole Gundersen own a steam sawmill in partnership. It cost about $6,000, but whether the proceeds will come up to expecta-tions cannot yet be determined exactly, as it was started only last fall, and this winter — a most unfortunate one for Texas — has had a paralyzing influence on all business. In fact we have had more cold and snow than anyone in this area can remember. In November it was very warm and trees and plants were in luxuriant growth, when we had a sudden severe frost one night. In the evening it was still so warm that it was uncomfortable to use a blanket; in the morning,

United States in 1839 and immediately took up missionary work among the Norwe-gian settlements in Illinois and Wisconsin. He was the first Norwegian Lutheran pastor to be ordained in this country. Eielsen was of a determined and bellicose nature and engaged in numerous skirmishes with other Norwegian pastors. He organized the so-called Ellingian Brotherhood (Eielsen Synod) and was its president from 1846 until his death. For full accounts of his life, see Christoffer O. Brohaugh and Ingvald Eisteinsen, *Kortfattet beretning om Elling Eielsens liv og virksomhed* (Chicago 1883) ; E. O. Mørstad, *Elling Eielsen og den "evangelisk-lutherske kirke" i Amerika* (Minne-apolis, 1917).

cabbage, wheat, turnips, fruit trees, and the like were frozen — things which never used to freeze here. Not only were the leaves frozen but entire trees of the more delicate varieties, such as pears, figs, and mulberries, and some grapevines, were killed by the frost. Many may sprout from the roots again, but we'll get no fruit from them this year and probably none next year.

We had snow four times this winter, and three times it remained on the ground for several days. The poor starving cattle, which had nothing to eat, were nearly covered with ice. A great many cattle, pigs, and sheep died, and people have had a very costly lesson, not to be so completely unconcerned about the winter season. I don't know a single person who had so much as stacked his straw. All of us left it on the ground, where it spoiled. We still do not know for sure how much we have lost, for we have not yet collected our live-stock. Spring is very late this year, and the old saying, "While the grass grows, the cows die," has been literally fulfilled, for most of the cattle died after the grass began to grow.

But to return to the mill — it is both a sawmill and a flour mill, and it runs well, but business has been slack this winter, for the oxen have been, and still are, in such poor condition that they can't be worked much. But now there will soon be an abundance of grass, the oxen will surely gain strength, and the lumber piles will vanish. All goods must be transported by oxcart, and most of those who come for lumber have a long way to haul it. They are reluctant to feed the oxen corn and will wait until there is enough grass along the road.

My husband has a third interest in the mill. He spends as much time there as at home, and this very evening he has undertaken a new job, namely to build the courthouse (the building in which legal cases are heard) for $6,000. This will mean still more traveling for him, but of course he hopes to profit very well from it.

About five weeks ago three farmer boys from Jutland came here direct from Denmark. One of them is working for us this summer, while another wants to work at the mill, where laborers earn $16 a month plus board. Three young men from Christiania also came, one of whom started working at the mill. They had spent three years in Wisconsin.

Many who had no work in Norway are doing fairly well here. There are nineteen Norwegian families in our settlement. They are all satisfied, and I know of no one who wishes he were back in Norway again. They are all prospering. My husband recently had a letter from a man who left here for Wisconsin. He says that he often admits to himself that he was a fool for selling his land and moving away from Texas. There is scarcely any doubt that it is now more profitable to settle here rather than in the Northern states, judging by the opinion of all those who come from there.

[ELISE WÆRENSKJOLD]

Ignorant of Religion[14]

PRAIRIEVILLE P.O.
KAUFMAN COUNTY, TEXAS
March 25, 1860

DEAR MOTHER-IN-LAW AND SISTERS-IN-LAW:

Since my husband has already written you several sheets, I have practically nothing to tell you this time, but I still want to send you a few lines to show you that I too have the best intentions. I do not know if Wilhelm has told you that last November the little boys and I went with him to Brownsboro, partly to see the mill and partly to visit my old acquaintances there. I had not seen my friends there for more than six years, although Brownsboro is only a day's journey from Prairieville. The trip was quite pleasant.

Not so very pleasant was the fact that Niels and Thorvald suffered attacks of whooping cough and were both quite sick during Christmas. They were not so ill, however, that they could not be up and about, but as I feared that others might contract the disease from them, I did not dare go anywhere with them during the win-

[14] Wilhelm's parents, Otto Christian Wærenskjold and Cathrine Caroline Poulsen, had two daughters, Nora Emilie Cecelie (Emilie), who married Oscar Syvertsen, and Otilde Fredrikke Elisabeth (Betha), who married Adolph S. Wattner. In the spring of 1870 the Wattners left Norway for New York, and went on to Texas the next year. In 1884 Emilie Syvertsen, then a widow, arrived in Texas with her son Oscar (later called Oscar W. Severson); he was the donor, in 1929, of this group of family letters, which are in the archives of the Norwegian-American Historical Association.

ter. Recently I have tried to wean Thorvald from his mother's milk. It has not been easy for either of us to do this, but it had to be done sometime, and I thought that it would be the best thing for both of us. The maid I had last winter is about to leave me now, and the new one arrived two weeks ago. This was the main reason why I wanted to wean Thorvald just now, for during this time Berthe, whom he loves so much, has plenty of time to look after him.

Niels speaks often of his aunts and little cousin [*Fanny Syvertsen*]— his "girl." He cried all this afternoon because his father got rid of an old mare that he [*Niels*] said was his. It did not console him at all that he got a younger and better mare and a gold dollar in exchange for the old horse, for his mare was to give birth to a colt next month and the new one is not in foal.

I suppose Wilhelm has told you that Otto and Niels go to Sunday school, where they are taught the catechism and the Bible. Niels said, "That school is fun," the first time he attended. It was certainly needed here, for many children have grown up completely ignorant of the teachings of religion. It was started by Pastor Eielsen, who visited us last winter. Perhaps you have heard people talk about him, and hardly in a complimentary manner; he is a Haugean who was ordained in Wisconsin. But he is a capable and unselfish man, untiring in his religious work. He is not trying to make money on his religion, and his behavior shows that he does not consider himself better than others, which our former pastor [*Fridrichsen*] did. He has now returned to his home in Wisconsin.

I would be very happy to hear from you soon and to learn that you are all well. Otto, Niels, and Thorvald send their love to Grandmother, to their dear aunts, to Uncle and the little cousin, and, by the way, I suppose that we ought not to forget Grandfather, though you never mention him.[15]

Much love from your devoted daughter-in-law and sister-in-law,

ELISE WÆRENSKJOLD

[15] "Grandfather" was presumably Wilhelm's stepfather. His own father died in 1836.

PART TWO

Trials of Reconstruction

1865–1875

We Count Ourselves Lucky [1]

[PRAIRIEVILLE
Late Summer or
Early Fall, 1865]

[TO A FRIEND IN CHRISTIANSAND:]

I suppose I should also tell a little about how we lived during the war. God be praised, I can say that we got along far better than one might have expected, though not always as we may have wished. During these years I frequently realized, with thankfulness, how much better God knows than we what determines our welfare. I had so often wished that my sons were older, which they might very well have been, considering my age (I am fifty); but what an inexpressible blessing it proved to be that they were young boys whom the conscription law could not touch! I would rather have left Texas a beggar than have had my children fight to preserve slavery. My husband was in the army three times, but never in any battle.

This very moment I was interrupted when a whole group of men passed by with three prisoners — people who, during the war, were very zealous in persecuting Union men. Two of them acted as executioners last year when three Union men were hanged without benefit of law or justice. Union men were those who did not favor secession

---

[1] This letter, obtained through the efforts of Derwood Johnson, reached the editor after the manuscript was set up in type. Although unsigned, it clearly was written by Elise Wærenskjold. It appeared in *Kristianssands stiftsavis*, December 25, 1865, with this prefaced remark by the editor: "From a letter from a lady in Texas to a local lady . . . we reprint the following sections, which we think will be read with interest."

of the Southern states from the union with the North. Practically all
the Norwegians were Union men. Many Union sympathizers were
killed or otherwise maltreated. At present the shoe is on the other
foot, but I hope that matters will now proceed according to law. I
hate and abhor all lawless acts. My husband and three other Norwegians were arrested at the same time (Whitsunday, 1864) as the
three Americans who were hanged. There were three hangmen, but
one escaped. One of the prisoners is a pastor. What do you think of
that? Is it not a noble thing for a minister to be an executioner?

During the war we always had plenty of money, but it was not
worth much. The rate was 20 paper dollars to one in gold; but usually
we bartered goods. Wool was my best medium of exchange. We
now have 278 sheep. All retail trade came to a stop during the war.
Toward the end, to be sure, some goods came in from Mexico, but
at exorbitant prices. One yard of cotton cloth cost from 15 to 20 paper
dollars; 1 pound of coffee, $20; 1 pound of sugar, $10; etc. Our products sold at the old prices: one pound of wool, $.20; 1 bushel of wheat
(¼ *tønde*), $1 in gold or twenty times as much in paper money.
Everyone had to spin and weave because not only the family at home,
but also the relatives in the army, had to be supplied with clothes, as
the government did not provide for them. Sometimes soldiers in the
service went about barefoot and in their underpants when their relatives did not have a chance to send them clothes.

Our government was despotic and dishonest, and the press told us
the grossest lies about victories that we did not win, and even about
battles that were never fought. If an editor had told us the truth, he
undoubtedly would have been killed. Those who would not fight
for the rebel government were in danger of their lives and were
subjected to all kinds of torture when caught. Great fraud was perpetrated in connection with the monetary system and with the "sub-
stitute law," which was put into effect simultaneously with the conscription law. The former act permitted a man to hire someone to
take his place in the army, provided the replacement was not subject
to conscription. But after the authorities had got a great number of
substitutes into the army, they abolished the law, forcing the men to
remain in the service, and then conscripted those who had hired the
substitutes at high prices. Men were not only compelled to go to war,

but many were literally dragged, yes, dragged off in chains, to the army.

The states where the war was fought suffered terribly from our own armies and from the armies of the enemy. But, God be praised, our part of the country escaped this double visitation, and consequently endured far less. To be sure, we have been left with many widows, orphans, and cripples; and those families that did not have slaves endured great hardships, as women and children had to do all the work because they could not hire Negroes at the exorbitant wages demanded by their owners. (I hired a man for $1,600 and three yards of woolen cloth, besides clothes for him: that is to say, three pairs of pants, two pairs of underpants, three shirts, three pairs of socks, a coat, a hat, and shoes. These clothes would have cost at least $750 if I had bought them.) But we were spared all plundering, and seeing our houses and fences burned by the soldiers, calamities which befell numerous families in other states. It is with reason, therefore, that we count ourselves lucky for being in Texas — so long as we had to be in a slave state. Since the war broke out I have frequently regretted that we settled in slave territory.

Until the war I did not really know the laws on slavery; but I know now that according to these laws I was guilty of penitentiary offenses more than a hundred times, because the law decreed several years of penal servitude only for saying in a private conversation that slavery was unjust. The same punishment was stipulated for helping a fugitive slave in any way; for example, giving him a meal, a night's lodging, or similar aid. Now the slaves are finally free, but as yet their freedom does not mean very much because their former owners try to scare them into remaining, and many of them have actually been killed. Some, however, have left their masters, or the latter have voluntarily sent them on their way. But what of the thousands of people who have nothing with which to make a start in life — many even lacking the clothes they need to cover their bodies? For great numbers of them, life will be harsher now than when they were slaves. Practically all the Norwegians have hired Negroes, and among us they are well treated.

We had to pay very high taxes during the war, but they were paid in paper money; in addition, one tenth of everything we raised or produced. The government impressed all imaginable products that were needed by the army, and at prices fixed by the authorities, which amounted to about a fourth of the real value of the goods. The government owes B[*ache?*] from Lillesand $10,000 — of which he will not receive five cents. Matters would have been somewhat tolerable if only the impressed goods had gone to the soldiers, but there was the most shameless profiteering on the part of officials, from the highest to the lowest government employee. Many families lost considerably during the war, which is only to be expected.

But I suppose you have had more than enough of politics; therefore to something else. [Johan] Reinert Reiersen, the former editor of *Christianssandsposten*, died a little more than a year ago of fever, after a few days' illness. He is survived by a sorrowing widow and four sons from his first marriage. The oldest, Oscar, who studied law, lives in Virginia, where he married a rich girl. The second [*John*] was a lieutenant, the third a soldier, in the Confederate Army. The youngest son was born here. The three youngest are now at home with the stepmother.

Texas has changed considerably during the last years. Much of the grass yielded to all sorts of weeds that the animals cannot eat. Consequently, we have suffered great depletions among our stock. In the winter of 1861–62 about 30 cattle died; the winter before last, 47; and last winter, about 20. To this must be added an equal number of calves — because the cows died just as they were about to calve — and also some young animals. Last year we also lost a number of sheep; but many people lost, proportionately, more cattle and sheep than we did. We could have been rich if conditions had continued as they were a decade ago. As things are now, we would gladly move, but this cannot be done, since it is impossible to sell for money.

[ELISE WÆRENSKJOLD]

I Long to See You All Again[2]

[PRAIRIEVILLE P. O.]
November 18, 1865

DEAR SISTERS-IN-LAW:

Since I cannot induce Wilhelm to write to you, I shall again send a few lines, as I am afraid that you did not receive the two letters I wrote you during the war. I hope, however, that you have heard from us indirectly, because I wrote to several people in Christiania after the coming of peace; namely, to Commissioner Anton Schjøth, Customs Officer Hans Franck, and Madams Franck, Basberg, and Stranger, and I asked Mr. Schjøth to convey our greetings to you. If you receive this letter, please give my regards to Schjøth and Franck and ask them to address their letters to me in the following manner: Mrs. Elise Wærenskjold, care of Mr. Elef Albertsen, Tyler, Smith County, Texas. We still do not have any mail service here, and God only knows when we will. But there are post offices in all the larger towns. Please ask Franck to notify the ladies of my address.[3]

If Schjøth received my letter, you will know how we lived during the war and that Wilhelm had some trouble as a result of the struggle. Fortunately all this is over and done with now; he has completely regained his health and has obtained a small position which, however, pays him practically nothing. The children have almost completely recovered too. Otto has been well all summer; the only thing he suffered from the snake bite was a big shock. Niels and Thorvald, also, have been cured of their fever, but Thorvald suffers daily from toothache as a result of all the calomel the doctors gave him when he was feverish. It is a good thing that he has not shed his teeth yet. How many times I have wished that we had as good doctors here as we had in Norway! As for me, I am feeling well, as usual; and though

² As has been mentioned, the letters written by Elise to her husband's family are in the archives of the Norwegian-American Historical Association. Brackets throughout this letter indicate that the original is so badly damaged that parts are illegible. The words within the brackets have been supplied by the editor and must be accepted as conjecture.

³ Anton Christian Gunerus Schjøth, 1807–72, was chief clerk in the Norwegian audit department after 1839. Trained both in law and in business, he was a teacher at the Christiania Institute of Business. From 1844–47 he was editor of a temperance newspaper. See a sketch by Einar Boyesen, in *Norsk biografisk leksikon,* 12:422.

I have always enjoyed fairly good health, I feel even better here than when I lived in Norway.

Dear sisters-in-law, it would make me very happy to hear from you soon and learn how you are. Do we not have a new brother-in-law, dear Otilde? [4] And how large is your family now, dear Emilie? How are old Grandmother and her husband getting along? I imagine she would be very happy if she could see her three Texas grandsons, and it is my own fervent wish that this may come about. For my interest in my ever-beloved native land and all my precious friends and relatives is as strong as when I left Norway, and I often long to see you all again. Unfortunately Wilhelm does not share this desire, so I am afraid that we shall never return to Norway. I know, of course, that such a trip would cost a great deal and that money is very difficult to get hold of. Still, I believe it would be possible to procure the necessary amount if only Wilhelm cared to go. Be that as it may, if God sees that this journey would be for our good, I think it will come about.

Otto is sitting by me as I write and tells me to give his love to Grandmother and his aunts. He says that he will write to you next year. He is the best-looking of our boys. The children learned little or nothing during these war years, as we had no school and there were so many other things to take care of. School has been held here since last spring; but it has now been interrupted for almost four months because a new school building is being erected. Though this building is ugly beyond description, it takes a very long time to complete it. God only knows how our husbands can be so indifferent toward a project that is of such great importance to our children. In a society where community spirit is lacking, nothing can thrive and prosper.

I did not lack help during the war, as many families did whose menfolk were fighting in the army. I had a very able German maid all the time and, in addition, a Negro woman a good deal of the time. We usually rented out the farm or else hired a Negro to work it for us. The mulatto whom we hired last year is still with us. We pay him $10 a month; but then, he is very capable and trustworthy. I suppose you know that the Negroes are free now. Of course this is a good thing for many of them, but, for awhile at least, things are going to be more difficult than they used to be for many women with small

---

[4] Otilde Fredrikke Elisabeth Wærenskjold's husband was Adolph C. Wattner.

children. Think of it, my dears! So many thousands of people suddenly left to their own resources without anything to give them a start in life! They have hardly enough clothes to cover their bodies— and this in a country terribly devastated by the war! Possibly this is not the case in Texas, but it is true of most of the other slave states.

I hope you will soon send us a very long letter. For five long years now we have heard nothing from Norway. I received four letters on the eve of the outbreak of the war, and I did not even have time to answer them before all delivery of mail was stopped. Since peace was declared we have had no mail service at all in the smaller towns, and the nearest post office is in Tyler, some fifty miles from here.

Prices of all agricultural products, with the exception of cotton, are very low. It is practically impossible to get any ready cash. This summer we have sold eighty-two wethers at $3 a head, but we have not received one cent of the money yet. Later we sold fifteen head of oxen, and all we have received for them thus far is $25. But I hope that after awhile conditions will improve, when things settle down after all the upheavals caused by the war, and when we grow more accustomed to the new relationship between the colored people and the whites. Many wealthy families suffered terrible losses through the emancipation of the Negroes; I know of a man who lost $200,000 by the change. Much as I have always wished for the Negroes to be free, I cannot help thinking that it would have been better, for them too, if their emancipation had been brought about a little more gradually. I should be very much interested in seeing what [the papers] at home say about developments in the United States in recent years. Almost all the S[candinavians] were opposed to the rebellion. The most determined rebels [have moved] away to other places where they are not so well [known]. [Had] they been victorious, the rest of us would have been forced to [leave].

Wilhelm greets you sincerely. He says he [hopes] we will get a post office in our county, but God knows when [this will happen]. The children also send you their warmest regards. Thorvald asks me to tell Grandmother that [he is going to raise] turkeys. They are very easy to raise [in their] natural habitat. Otto is very fond of [fishing and] hunting; he shot a deer and a turkey this fall, besides some smaller animals and birds. Niels, on the other hand, prefers to ride about looking after the cattle and the hogs, a very useful and necessary occupation for a Texas farmer.

Hoping soon to receive good news from all of you, I conclude by sending my best greetings to Grandmother and her husband, to you, dear sisters-in-law, to Mr. [Oscar] Syvertsen, and to all the children. Farewell to all, and do write soon to your devoted

[ELISE WÆRENSKJOLD]

The News Is Very Sad

VAN ZANDT COUNTY, TEXAS
February 2, 1866

DEAR SISTERS-IN-LAW:

This time the news I have for you is very sad. It has pleased the Lord to take from us the dearest thing we possessed on this earth, our most beloved child Thorvald. Of course, I love all my children beyond words; but Thorvald was so much younger than the others, and he was such a sweet, lovely child that he was his father's and his mother's favorite. Both he and Niels fell ill in the month of July; I believe that from that time the disease which finally caused his death was in his body, although he apparently had recovered. A week ago last Sunday, on January 21, we walked over to one of our neighbors after dinner, and Thorvald ran beside me, happy and gay as usual. After we had stayed a couple of hours with our friends, I had to go home to bring in the sheep, and I asked if any of the others felt like walking home with me; but they said they wanted to stay on a little longer. Only my sweet little Thorvald wanted to go with Mama. On the way home he chatted with me as was his wont, and there was not the slightest indication that anything was wrong with him. We had taken hardly more than ten steps, however, after his last words, when suddenly, without uttering a sound, he collapsed beside me. When I looked at him I could see that he had the cramps. I picked him up in my arms and carried him home as fast as I could and sent for Wilhelm and the doctor.

Thorvald was ill three days, and I am afraid he suffered a great deal. On the third day he spoke a little, but it was very difficult for him to pronounce the words distinctly. I was so unspeakably happy when he began to talk on Wednesday morning, for I began then to hope that God might still let me keep my dear child. But no, it was not to be; about noon he began to breathe more heavily, and around four o'clock he died. He was buried on Friday of that week.[5]

I know that my little Thorvald now is happy with God—surely much happier than we could ever have made him here on earth—but I miss him so terribly. Yet I am calm and composed in my grief, for like David I know that my boy can never come back to me, but sometime I shall go to him—and that time cannot be very far off because in a few days I shall be fifty-one years old. When I was very young, I felt that I would be happy to die whenever it should please the Lord to call me to him, but since the children came, I have wanted to live for them. Now one of the strongest ties that bound me to life here on earth has been severed, and I feel so much more drawn toward Heaven. Thorvald was a blessing to me as long as he was alive, and I now hope that in the loving wisdom of God his going, too, may prove to be a blessing for me and mine. His death was a call from God, a forceful reminder to us to be prepared for death and judgment, and I hope we shall never forget it. The life we live here is not a very spiritual one. We think far too much of earthly things and lack all concrete reminders of the existence of God's heavenly kingdom. It is sad to be without divine service and religious instruction, especially for the younger generation. Our children are now almost old enough to be confirmed, but there are no prospects that they actually will be.

Please let my dear, highly esteemed friend, Royal Commissioner Schjøth, read this. Just now I cannot write more than this letter and one to my own relatives. Since peace was declared I have written to you, to Schjøth, to Customs Officer Franck, to his wife, to the wife of Customs Officer Basberg, and to many others, but I still have not received a single line in reply from anyone. Give our best to Mr. Syvertsen and your mother, and accept many greetings from all of us, especially from your devoted

[ELISE WÆRENSKJOLD]

[5] Thorvald was seven years old at the time of his death.

P.S. Wilhelm and the children are well. The death of our dear little Thorvald was a very heavy blow to Wilhelm. Write after my name: Care of Mr. Elef Albertsen, Tyler, Smith County, Texas, United States of America.

My Thorvald Is Gone

FOUR MILE PRAIRIE
June 22, 1866

To MRS. THOMINE DANNEVIG:

You undoubtedly know that my sweet little Thorvald is gone. This was so absolutely unexpected and came so suddenly, like lightning from a clear sky. Our neighbor's daughter had her wedding January 19, and because their house was very small and they wished to invite about two hundred guests, they asked to have the wedding in our house. Perhaps the abundance of cakes and fresh meat that were provided for the occasion, which lasted several days, was harmful to Thorvald. Yet he didn't seem to be ill. Sunday afternoon, January 21, several people who were staying with us, my husband, Thorvald, and I went over to visit a Danish family who live a mile and a half from us. When I wanted to go home to bring in the sheep, all the others thought it was too early; but Thorvald wanted to go along home with Mama and on the way chatted quite cheerfully with me. We had gone only some ten steps after he last spoke when, without a complaint, without a sound, he sank down at my side. He spoke no more until Wednesday morning, when he regained consciousness and could speak a few words and give Mama a last kiss. I was so happy then, for I believed he would recover, but that was not to be. At four o'clock he died; he was buried on Friday. Yes, little did I think the Friday before, when the house was filled with gay wedding guests, that the next Friday I should lose the dearest treasure I had on earth. My little Thorvald was such a sweet, lovable boy, and all who knew him loved him. I cannot really enjoy anything, and my only desire is to be with my Thorvald once more. I must, however, tell you of a strange question that my little Tulli (which is what he called himself) asked me the night before he took sick, just as though he had a premonition of his impending death. He asked me if I didn't think it would be too bad if he died now. Because I didn't think there was the slightest danger that such a thing could happen, I was merely surprised and asked why. "Oh," he said, "if I died I would always keep this bad breath which I have just now." His idea was that the new body we get after death would be exactly like the one we leave when we die. I told him that our new body in all probability will have a certain likeness to our earthly one, but that it will be free of all defects and imperfections. He then asked me many things about resurrection and the next life, much more than I was able to explain to him. Now my little angel knows all that he wished to know—and all that is still a mystery to us. Otto and Niels are well. If only they could learn something and be confirmed!

A little over $300 a year has been subscribed here for the salary of a minister, and a letter has been written to a Norwegian pastor in Illinois, Rasmussen, to procure one for us—with what success remains to be seen.[6]

[ELISE WÆRENSKJOLD]

I Have Lost My Husband[7]

FOUR MILE PRAIRIE
April 15, 1867

DEAR THORVALD:

When this letter arrives, you will doubtless have heard that I have lost my husband, the loving father of my children. Only God knows which of us will be next. If I should be taken from the children before Otto, at least, is of age, it would be very hard for them in many ways. However, God's will be done! It does no good to worry about what may happen. It would be quite different if I were in Norway, for

[6] Peter Andreas Rasmussen, famous pioneer pastor (1829–98), was born in Stavanger, Norway, and emigrated to the United States in 1850. He was minister at Lisbon, Illinois, at the time of this letter.
[7] This letter to Commodore Thorvald Dannevig was published in Tønsbergs blad, May 18, 1925, together with the series written to his mother, Mrs. Dannevig. See ante, part 1, n. 7.

there I have both relatives and faithful friends whom I know I could count on. Here I am alone in a foreign land where I have no assurance that anyone would assume the responsibility of providing a Christian training for my children or of safeguarding their inheritance. During the war my husband made a will, so I have full authority over everything and can administer our affairs as I see fit.[8]

Old [Erick] Bache has left us too. His widow is well provided for. But it is unfortunate that she cannot sell out and return to Norway. That is not possible now unless one is willing to sell for a half or a third of what property was worth before the war.

Thank you so much for the photographs. Is it not possible also to get pictures of landscapes, or is the price prohibitive? I would like to have a view of Lillesand and of my birthplace, the Dybvaag parsonage. You have likely seen it from the sea. I was eight years old when we moved from there, but I remember every detail so clearly, even better than I remember Moland or Holt, where we lived later.[9]

We subscribe to three newspapers—a Norwegian, a German, and an English one. I rarely have an opportunity to read any French except in the French books I brought from Norway.

Recently Oscar Reiersen returned from New Orleans and Shreveport, where he had visited an uncle. Although Oscar was only a little boy when he came to America, he has retained a greater interest in everything Norwegian than any other member of the Reiersen family.[10]

April 30

I must tell you something about the western Norwegian settlement in Bosque County. Not long ago Indians descended upon it; they wounded an old Norwegian, and carried off a fifteen-year-old boy. In addition they took two American boys whose father they had killed, and they also killed two Negroes. No doubt the Bosque settlement is richer than ours and, I think, also more healthful, but still I wouldn't for the world live so near the Indians.

[8] For an account of Wærenskjold's death, which actually occurred November 17, 1866, see Introduction, page 14.

[9] Mrs. Wærenskjold later obtained water-color paintings of Lillesand harbor, and of the parsonages at West Moland and Holt. See Introduction, n. 7.

[10] The uncle in Shreveport was Georg Reiersen of the firm of Reiersen and Grøgaard. In 1894 Oscar Reiersen sent Mrs. Wærenskjold an account of his family's journey from Norway to Texas, which she quoted in a letter to *Amerika* written in 1894, to follow in part 4 of the present series.

It was hard to bury little Thorvald, but it would be much harder to know that he was among wild, heathen people who would torture him every day and bring him up as a pagan. Very soon a few poems that my husband wrote on the occasion of our Thorvald's death will be sent to your uncle. I thought it might interest my friends to read them.

[ELISE WÆRENSKJOLD]

Parties in Prairieville [11]

[PRAIRIEVILLE P. O.
Summer, 1868?]

DEAR MADAM STAACK:

You can imagine that I was not a little surprised to see Niels come home, long before I expected him. I was very happy when he was safely back again; but if I had known that my boy had undertaken such a long trip alone and that he had to sleep out in the open, I would have been very anxious. The horse was terribly skinny: I forgot to remind Niels that it had to be fed.

I have paid your tax, as you will see by the enclosed receipt. I have not seen Hansen yet, because he is sick. His sons disputed about his property when he came home. He is absolutely broke now, so there will be nothing to inherit. If I receive anything from [John S.] Martens, I shall let you know. I have not seen your brother [*Knud Hansen*] either.

All those who have the right to vote in our Norwegian Lutheran church, as well as all the married women, were here for dinner last Sunday (without a single cake or pie); but Knud Hansen did not

[11] The originals of the two letters in this collection addressed to Madam Staack have been presented to the association by Mrs. Clara Callan of Clifton, Texas. Both the heading and the conclusion of this letter are missing, hence we do not know the date. But it was evidently written after the death of Wilhelm Wærenskjold in 1866; Niels, who was born in 1853, is spoken of as a young, irresponsible boy. If we assume that he was about fifteen, the date of the letter would be 1868. This is corroborated by the last paragraph, which suggests that the violence of reconstruction days was rampant at the time of writing. Furthermore, there is mention of "the problem of getting a minister." The Four Mile congregation was organized in 1868, and the Reverend O. O. Estrem began his service there in 1869. On the Staacks, see *ante*, part 1, n. 8.

come. They got Ouline [Reiersen] to make a pledge for him, as the meeting concerned the problem of getting a minister.

I had a letter from Fredrikke, and, with it, special greetings to Madam Staack. They made the trip to Monroe in fifteen days and had no mishap during the journey. It seems that Marie is already dissatisfied, according to what George writes. He offers $100 for boarding her, and I have written that I am willing to take her.

We had a gay party in Prairieville, as Martin Schofstad can tell you. Otto was along. He wore knee breeches, a cotton blouse, and an Indian cap, which made him look so strange that I would not have recognized him if I had not known that it was he. All of them wore different kinds of costumes. During the night they danced. I have not seen so many people together in many years. At Schofstads' we had a very fine dinner party, with dancing for the young people. And at Andersens' we had a fine and very merry party Sunday, eight days ago. We are to have a party at Madam Bache's when Andreas [Staack?] and Emma arrive. You will see from this that we can still have some merriment on Four Mile.

Today my boys and Christian H[alvorsen?] are out cattle hunting on Twelve-Mile [Prairie]. I must tell you the happy news that I have been able to borrow enough money from one of my Norwegian friends to pay all my debts if my creditors will be a bit reasonable and let me pay the interest with produce. I heard from Norway that the money has been sent to the Norwegian consul in New Orleans. I have written to your brother-in-law [*I. I. Staack*] for you.[12] I suppose you have seen in the papers that Torgersen has gone to Quebec with a ship commanded by Captain Stranger (Hanna Holm's husband). I have not heard from him. Simon has had a letter from Hansen. His wife has had another little one. Mina is to be confirmed in the fall and Laura in the spring. This has been written by lamplight. Good night!

<hr/>

[12] I. I. Staack, brother of J. H. Staack (husband of Madam Staack), in a letter sent from Copenhagen of November 22, 1889, said that he and other heirs of "your Aunt Sophie" (Staack) in Denmark "have given our part toward the support of the deaf-mute Christian Staack in Lübeck. He is to have the interest on the money left by Aunt Sophie as long as he lives, and after his death the capital goes to Fr. Wiebeck and his children in Bergedorff [*Bergedorf*]." A rather desperate letter, apparently from J. H. Staack, went to a cousin in Europe, saying that after three bad years, the writer needed help, and requesting that the estate go through the usual legal procedures; but he never received any share in it. A copied letter given the Norwegian-American Historical Association by Mrs. C. E. Price; Mrs. Price to the editor, April 7, 1961.

Now you must write to me soon and give me all the news from Bosque, especially how you and your children are getting along. Tell me also how Niels behaved on the way and in Bosque. "Tiger" had much to relate when he came home, so I am afraid that someone behaved very badly. You must be sure to tell the truth. And please let me know about my old friends in Bosque, not forgetting Ole Halvorsen or the newcomers or Poulsen. Can he account for all the money he received from the Americans before he went to Norway? How is Madam Haagestøl getting along? Two of Madam Wilsen's stepsons shot a Negro, but I do not know if the wound was fatal. There has been much trouble at Jordan's Saline. One Negro was killed and all the others were deprived of their weapons and money. Several Union men fled from there, it is said.[13] . . .

[ELISE WÆRENSKJOLD]

An Egyptian Plague — Grasshoppers [14]

PRAIRIEVILLE P.O.
KAUFMAN COUNTY
September 29, 1868

To MRS. KAJA POPPE:

Health conditions have been excellent in our community this summer, but many of the old neighbors have left us and moved to Bosque, which is a more healthful district. It is also a better wheat-producing area, and there is always a good market for grain. I had sowed fifteen bushels of wheat, but the venture failed because we were struck by an Egyptian plague—grasshoppers. They came here toward the end of October and left us only when they had eaten up everything green. A most unusual spell of drought followed; we were unable to plant again until just before Christmas. Then, in the spring, came a new spawn of grasshoppers that ate the sprouting wheat. When they were big enough to fly, they disappeared. The wheat had cost me $50—

[13] Jordan's Saline is the present Grand Saline in Van Zandt County, Texas. The concluding sentence of the letter is illegible.
[14] This letter was published in *Tønsbergs blad*, May 19, 1925. Elise and Svend Foyn stayed in Mrs. Poppe's house in Lillesand immediately after their marriage; Hageland, in *Lillesands-posten*, December 28, 1922.

so it was a great loss. Moreover, I lost over half my sheep as a result of starvation, five horses, and twenty-seven milk cows, not to mention the colts. The dry grass, which the grasshoppers couldn't destroy, was burned by the prairie fires, causing us great trouble. I had never re-alized that grasshoppers could fly so high. The air was filled with them as far as one could see. Otherwise we have had a good harvest in Texas and also a good yield of fruit. I have harvested several hundred bushels of peaches. I imagine you know that a bushel equals one fourth of a *tønde*.

I must tell you that I have been without a maid now for almost a year, as my German girl, who had been with me for six years, left to join her brother in Louisiana. I get along quite well, however, and of course I save considerable money. During the months when the milking was heaviest, two Negro women milked with me in return for a little sweet and a little sour milk, which of course I did not miss. I have set aside about $50 worth of butter to sell. At present we milk only three cows; all the rest of the calves are now free to graze and fatten before winter comes.

For the next few months, I shall be able to lead a leisurely life. You no doubt know that I have leased my farm to some Negroes in re-turn for half of their crop. I would much rather have a white man by the year—if I could find a Norwegian. But since the war that is no longer possible. If any Norwegians do come to Texas, they all go to Bosque, which is now the largest Norwegian settlement in the state. On the whole, the Negroes conduct themselves very well—much bet-ter, in fact, than the white Americans.

Those people who are well situated in Norway have no reason for coming here. But I would consider it a great advantage for the many needy persons, including many on poor relief, to come to Texas.

[ELISE WÆRENSKJOLD]

Hard to Get Help

PRAIRIEVILLE P.O.
KAUFMAN COUNTY, TEXAS
June 9, 1869

DEAR SISTER-IN-LAW [*Emilie Syvertsen*]:

Today I had the unexpected joy of receiving your letter of April 6. Otto, who got it in Prairieville, was so surprised and curious to see a letter addressed to his father that he opened it. I thank you very much for the portraits. It is true that they are not as good as the others I have had from Norway, but I was still very happy to get them. Your sister [*Elisabeth Wattner*] is supposed to have sent me three letters, but I have not received them, and I imagine that your letter was lost with them. Since I wrote to tell you about my husband's death, I have had only one letter from the Wattners. In the letters I got in December, 1866 (which were written in September of that year), from your mother, your sister, and from Wattner to Wilhelm, they mentioned that you were going to write and send the portraits, and I waited and waited, but nothing came. I wrote only to Wattner after the death of my husband and asked him to relate this sad news to Wilhelm's mother and sisters.

I am happy to hear that you are well, but I had thought that you were getting along better than you are, and least of all expected to hear that you have no maid, with wages so low in Norway. Since Whitsuntide of this year I again have a maid; I must pay her $6 a month. Like you, I can get along without one during the winter, but unless I absolutely have to, I find it too strenuous to manage alone during the summer. How much do you harvest on your farm in an average year?

I hope that Oscar is quite well again now.[15] As you know, children usually recover rapidly, once they start getting better. It must have been a hard time for you, my dear Emilie. I imagine you have read the verses which your brother wrote on the occasion of the death of our dear little Thorvald. I know that he sent a copy of them back home. I have never felt quite happy since the deaths of Thor-

[15] Oscar Syvertsen, the younger. See part 1, n. 14.

vald and Wilhelm and have worn mourning ever since they died. I enclose a portrait of Otto and hope to be able to send you my own and Niels's later on, and also one of Thorvald. We have to travel fifty miles to get our pictures taken, so you can understand that it takes both time and money. I went to Tyler last fall, but there was no photographer there who was any good.

You talk about peasants living as cottagers. Such conditions are unknown here, where everybody, even the poorest Negro, is too self-sufficient to submit to such a state of dependence. It is even hard to get help for months at a time, because those who do not have land of their own prefer to rent. The owner of the land has to supply buildings, work animals, tools, and seeds; he also has to feed the animals and pay for the maintenance of the fences. In return for this, he gets half the harvest. It is mainly the freed Negro slaves who rent land in this way. Many of them are lazy, cruel to the animals, or so careless with the tools that they cause a lot of trouble.

This year we have twenty-two acres of cotton, fourteen of corn, six of rye, and seven of wheat. The rye and wheat have already been harvested. Plums and blackberries have been ripe for several weeks —early, is it not? Otto has eight acres of cotton, and what he can harvest on that piece of land, he is to have for himself. Niels's main job is to look after the cattle and the pigs. We have between two and three hundred hogs, and last winter we sold about $300 worth of hogs and bacon. We received $.05 per pound for live pork and $.11 per pound for the smoked bacon, and we have also sold some oxen and ninety-three wethers. Prices are $10 for a four-year-old ox and $1.50 for a wether. It used to be $3. In addition to this, I sold turkeys last fall and got $25 for them, all told. Now that I have paid off my debt, we manage fairly well. I do not know yet how things will work out with regard to the money that is owing to me. It is an annoying affair.

Please tell me how to address my letters if I want to send them directly to you. Grandmother is old now, and I do not imagine that she will live much longer. Is your aunt, Mrs. Poulsen, still living? Is it not true that your mother would inherit a considerable sum of money if she survives Mrs. Poulsen? I am happy that your little girl [Fanny] is good about writing. She shames my boys, who have not written to Grandmother yet. They have fallen behind a good deal because no school was held here during the war, and now they do not have much time.

I must not forget to tell you an important piece of news: we are to have a Norwegian pastor, namely, the Reverend [Ole Olsen] Estrem. He is from Illinois and was supposed to leave there in May. He is to live in Bosque County, where there are now more than sixty Norwegian families. We have only seventeen Norwegian families here. When he comes I hope to have Otto and Niels confirmed; that has been my wish for a long time. There are many married people in Texas who are not confirmed.[16]

And now, my dear Emilie, once again many thanks for your letter and the portraits, and many greetings to you, your husband, and children. Write again soon to your devoted

ELISE WÆRENSKJOLD

Send Data about Bosque [17]

PRAIRIEVILLE P.O.
KAUFMAN COUNTY, TEXAS
July 25, 1869

DEAR MR. QUÆSTAD:

Excuse me for taking the liberty of sending you these lines. Recently I had a letter from the editors of *Billed-magazin* in which

[16] The Reverend Ole Olsen Estrem was born near Haugesund, Norway, in 1835, and emigrated to the United States in 1857. He was ordained in 1862. He married Josephine Emilie Amundson the following year. He was pastor at Clifton, Texas, 1869–77, and after being a minister at Willmar, Minnesota, he returned to Texas and served at Waco, 1904–08. He died in July, 1910.

[17] A photostatic copy of this letter has been sent to the editor by Derwood Johnson. The original is in the possession of Mrs. Ole J. Hoel of Norse, Texas, a granddaughter of Carl Quæstad; she now lives on the original Quæstad farm. Carl Engebretson Quæstad was born in Hedmark, Norway, in 1815. He married Sedsel Olsdatter Ringnæs in 1841 and went to Kaufman County, Texas, ten years later, moving to Bosque County in 1853 or 1854. There he became a prosperous farmer and cattleman. He is said to have been a well-informed man with a wide circle of friends; he often aided newly arrived immigrants. His interest in the pioneers is evidenced by the fact that he was "the moving spirit in having a monument raised on Cleng Peerson's grave," a dream that he saw realized shortly before his death in 1886. He was buried in Norse, Texas, by the side of Peerson. See O. Canuteson, obituary of Carl Quæstad, in *Skandinaven*, February 23, 1887. The following inscription appears on Peerson's monument: "CLENG PEERSON, / The Pioner of Norse Emigration / to / AMERICA. / Born In Norway, Europe, / May 17, 1782. / Landed in America in 1821 / Died in Texas / December 18, 1865. / GRATEFUL COUNTRYMEN IN TEXAS / ERECTED THIS TO HIS MEMORY."

both of them asked me for a description of the Norwegian settlements in Texas; and one of them, Mr. Svein Nilsson, says that he
wants to visit us in the fall. By that time I would like to gather as
much information as possible. I therefore permit myself to ask you,
dear Mr. Quæstad, to be kind enough to send me all available data
about Bosque: when it was first settled and by whom; who arrived
later and from where; its present population; the physical nature
of the area and its products; how much can be raised per acre; in
short, anything which may be of interest. I assume you agree with
me that it would be to our own interest as well as to that of our
country and our many poor countrymen if a part of the migration
from the Scandinavian countries could be directed toward Texas. I
therefore hope you will be good enough to contribute whatever you
can toward this end.

You and your family as well as our other friends in Bosque are
greeted most heartily from the boys and

Yours sincerely,
ELISE WÆRENSKJOLD

A New Home in America [18]

[PRAIRIEVILLE P. O
Autumn, 1869?

TO THE EDITOR:

For some time several persons in the district of Christiansand ha
been giving special attention to the emigration problem. Then the
learned that Johan Reinert Reiersen, the editor of *Christianssand*

[18] This account of the founding of the earliest Norwegian settlements in Texas wa
published in *Billed-magazin* (Madison, Wisconsin), 2:58–60, 66, 75 (February 19, 26
March 5, 1870). This periodical, edited by Svein Nilsson, represented one of the fir
attempts to publish a popular Norwegian magazine in the United States, and, lik
many later ventures, it proved to be short-lived, running for only two years, 1868–7
Nevertheless, it has proved an invaluable source for students interested in Norwegia
immigrant history. A photostatic copy of the article was furnished by the Minneso
Historical Society. Files of *Billed-magazin* are owned by the Minnesota Historical So
ciety and Luther College of Decorah, Iowa. See D. G. Ristad, "Svein Nilsson, Pione
Norwegian-American Historian," in *Norwegian-American Studies and Records*, 9:29
37 (Northfield, 1936); Johannes B. Wist, ed., *Norsk-amerikanernes festskrift 191*
(Decorah, Iowa, [1914]).

posten, wanted to seek a new home in America. The people believed that in him they had found the right man to study conditions over there and give a report about them. At the suggestion of Christian Grøgaard, son of Pastor [Hans Jacob] Grøgaard in Bergen (author of the *Læsebog*) he [*Reiersen*] was requested to make the trip unencumbered by his family so that he could visit the various states where conditions might seem favorable for Norwegian settlements. Upon his return he could then give a complete report about these areas. For such an undertaking he was offered three hundred *speciedaler*. Reiersen accepted the offer, and in the summer of 1843 he left Norway by way of Havre de Grace, France, for the port of New Orleans.[19]

From there he went to the Northwestern states, where he visited the already established Norwegian settlements, and then he wrote a brief account of his impressions. This was sent from Galena [Illinois] to Hans Gasmann, who added his own remarks as an appendix.[20] Pastor Unonius and several Norwegians at Pine Lake and Wiota [Wisconsin] confirmed Reiersen's report. All this was included in *Veiviser for norske emigranter* [Guide for Norwegian Emigrants] that Reiersen published after his return in 1844. He also traveled through Texas, at that time an independent republic, and wrote a very favorable description of the country, which may be found in *Veiviser*, page 136 and following.[21]

[19] For information about John Reinert Reiersen, see Introduction, p. 3. Hans Jacob Grøgaard (1764–1836) became well known as minister, educator, and member of the Eidsvold convention. His mildly rationalistic *Læsebog for børn* (Reader for Children), a retelling of the Bible story, was first published in Christiania in 1816. He was pastor at West Moland, 1811–23, and then at Bergen, where he served until his death.

[20] Hans Gasmann (1787–1861) was a prominent figure in early Norwegian immigrant history. He settled at Pine Lake, Wisconsin, in 1843. His emigration caused much surprise, as he was considered prosperous and had been twice elected to the Storting (parliament) from his district, Gjerpen. See Anderson, *Norwegian Immigration*, 358; Blegen, *Norwegian Migration, 1825–1860*, 135, 151, 206–208. Mrs. Wærenskjold's letter, as originally printed, erroneously gave the name as Mons Gasman.

[21] Gustaf Elias Unonius (1810–1902) founded the first Swedish settlement in the Midwest. He was born of a well-to-do official family and was educated at Uppsala University in Sweden. In 1841 he settled at New Upsala near Pine Lake, Wisconsin. He was ordained an Episcopal minister in 1845. He moved to Chicago in 1849 and organized a Scandinavian congregation; he also served as Norwegian-Swedish consul. He returned to Sweden in 1858. His memoirs, published at Uppsala in 1861–62, are among the most valuable ever written by a Scandinavian immigrant. They have been translated and edited by Jonas Oscar Bachlund and Nils William Olsson under the title *A Pioneer in Northwest America, 1841–1858: The Memoirs of Gustaf Unonius* (2 volumes, Minneapolis, 1950, 1960). Reiersen's famous guidebook was widely read and did much to stimulate emigration from Norway. See Introduction, n. 1.

In March, 1845, Reiersen left Lillesand, accompanied by Christian Grøgaard and Syvert Nielsen, a smith's apprentice from Birkenes Parish. At Havre de Grace they were met by Reiersen's father, Ole Reiersen, the former sexton at Holt, with his oldest daughter [Lina] and his son [Gerhard] the watchmaker, together with Stiansen, a carpenter from Christiansand. The latter had gone by way of Arendal, as they could not all sail on the same vessel—it was too crowded. At Havre they boarded an American ship for New Orleans, and it was not until their arrival there that they definitely decided to go to Texas, which they now learned would be admitted to the Union. While still at home they had agreed that they wanted to choose a milder climate than that of Wisconsin, but they wavered between Missouri and Texas.

In New Orleans Sexton Reiersen bought a land certificate for 1,476 acres entitling him to choose that amount of unclaimed land anywhere in Texas. He also received a letter of introduction from the Texas consul to Dr. Starr in Nacogdoches (the oldest town in Texas), requesting his help in staking out the purchased land.[22] Among the Norwegians whose acquaintance they made in New Orleans, James Trumpy of Bergen must be mentioned. He still lives there and carries on an important and flourishing business. This man has shown unusual generosity toward the Norwegian immigrants and has several times assisted them with money when they had too little to reach Texas.

From New Orleans they continued by steamer up the Mississippi and Red rivers to Natchitoches, from where old Reiersen, the editor himself [*J. R.*], and Lina Reiersen went overland to Nacogdoches, arriving on the Fourth of July. Since we so often read in Scandinavian papers that the "poor whites" (which by Texan standards would include practically all Norwegian immigrants) are treated with contempt and arrogance, I cannot refrain from quoting several lines from Editor Reiersen's letter:

[22] James Harper Starr (1809–90) was appointed president of the board of land commissioners and receiver of the land dues for Nacogdoches County when the Texas General Land Office was created in 1837. He and his assistants performed their duties so well that on several occasions they were threatened with mob violence by dishonest speculators. In 1844 he became joint director of a land office in Nacogdoches. In Mrs. Wærenskjold's letter of August 25, 1894, to follow, his name is spelled incorrectly as "Starn." Information about Starr was furnished by the Texas State Historical Association at Austin. The consul represented the republic of Texas in New Orleans.

FROM A PORTRAIT OWNED BY HIS GREAT-GRANDSON,
R. W. REIERSON OF HOUSTON, TEXAS

J. R. Reiersen

Lillesand harbor

Holt parsonage, near Arendal

The Wærenskjold family: Wilhelm, Elise, Otto, and Niels

Cleng Peerson's monument at Norse, Texas

Elise Wærenskjold

Four Mile Church, built 1875

SKETCHED BY MRS. JOEL E. NELSON FROM A SNAPSHOT MADE BY PASTOR R. J. MELAND

The Wærenskjold house at Four Mile Prairie

FROM A CALLING CARD OWNED BY MRS. WILLIAM WARENSKJOLD

Elise in later life

"We stopped at a restaurant run by a Mr. Miller, where we had a very good dinner after washing up and changing clothes. Directly after dinner I paid a visit to a German merchant, Mr. Hoya, who had the largest store in town. There I met another German, or rather a Schleswiger, by the name of Bondiz, who was also a merchant. They showed us every courtesy, and Mr. Hoya offered us any assistance in his power. He took me to see Dr. Starr (former finance minister under President Sam Houston), to whom I presented my letter of introduction. I found him to be a highly cultured, kindly, and excellent person in every respect, whose staunch and upright character was delineated in his face. He himself went with me to the land office to authenticate the certificate we had purchased, and we found everything in perfect order. He told me where vacant land was available and promised to introduce me to a reliable surveyor who was intimately acquainted with all the boundary marks.

"Well satisfied, I had no sooner returned and told my father that everything was in order when we were all invited to a ball that was to be held at the courthouse that same evening, and, despite the fact that we were poorly equipped with ball dress, we accepted. My sister [Lina], together with our host's ladies, was called for in a carriage at seven o'clock, while Father and I set out at the same time with Hoya. I had no great expectations so far as this party was concerned, and was therefore certainly surprised at the elegance of the planters, and even more so when our host presented us to the assembled and arriving guests. In general, however, their costumes were not particularly formal according to our strict rules of etiquette. 'General Rusk, Mr. Reiersen from Norway; Colonel Tom, Mr. Reiersen; Judge Sterne, Mr. Reiersen; Dr. Louis, Mr. Reiersen; Captain Walding, Mr. Reiersen'—and thus the presentation of generals, colonels, judges, and doctors proceeded until the whole party had made the acquaintance of 'Mr. Reiersen from Norway.'

"I looked around in amazement at this company of high-ranking persons dressed in light, varied summer attire, but could not discover the least trace of that superciliousness that usually characterizes our upper classes and betrays itself even in their poorly disguised condescension. Here everything was straightforward, free and easy, and soon I felt at home in this group of distinguished gentlemen from military and civilian life. I conversed easily, first with one and then the other, while the younger men danced so graciously with the ladies that it even won Father's approval. Such courteous and friendly behavior toward common strangers is extremely pleasant, and I shall not soon forget the Fourth of July, 1845."

The Reiersens remained in Nacogdoches several weeks, because the surveyor was unable to leave earlier for his district, which lay about ninety miles to the northwest. Their companions, Christian Grøgaard, Gerhard Reiersen, Stiansen, and Syvert Nielsen, had continued their journey up the Red River to Shreveport and thence overland to Marshall, Texas, where they stayed some time, the latter three having obtained work.

Now I should like briefly to relate what happened to Nielsen, so that people can understand how stupid it is for Norwegian newcomers to change their names. After he had worked awhile in Marshall, he joined the army as a blacksmith at $50 a month. As he was a frugal young man and earned a bit on the side by playing the violin, he let his pay accumulate as a fund to enable him to go back to Norway and get his parents, brothers, and sisters. A Mr. Crawford, whose acquaintance he had made in Marshall, talked with him in Austin (the capital of Texas); at that time he [Nielsen] had $1,500 due him from the American government. Soon afterward, he died on the way to El Paso. Crawford, who by chance came through Four Mile Prairie, asked a Norwegian living there to inform Nielsen's parents. This was done, but because he had Americanized his name, the Norwegian consul in New York, whom the parents had commissioned to collect the inheritance, could get nothing, since it was impossible to discover the name under which he had enlisted. Perhaps Crawford knew, but he had left Marshall, and the Norwegians did not know where he had gone.

Toward fall Reiersen went out to look for land and selected as his home a place several miles [west] of the Neches River, where no one had settled. Here they got their 1,476 acres surveyed, as well as a claim of 640 acres. At the same time a few American families and an old Norwegian bachelor, Knud Olsen, who had come from the Northern states, took land in the same vicinity. This was the first meager beginning of a Norwegian settlement in Texas.

After helping his father buy the necessary farm animals and start building a log house, J. R. Reiersen left for New Orleans to meet his wife and children, his mother, and his younger sister [Gina], besides a larger immigrant party expected from Norway. Only half of the party arrived, however.[23] The group had chartered two ships in Norway to take them to Havre de Grace, but a certain number who were to leave by schooner from Lillesand fell into disagreement with the owner over the rate, after which he would not let them lease his vessel on any condition. Consequently their journey had to be postponed until the next year. This substantially affected the emigration to Texas, because the leaders of the Lillesand party, Peder Nielsen Kalvehaven, Osuld Enge, and Anders Holte, three capable and upright men, had planned that Christian Grøgaard—who in his youth had studied theology and was a very well educated man—should be teacher and pastor for the future settlement. But, as already stated, this group was delayed in Norway, and when they finally arrived in New Orleans they went not to Texas but to Missouri, where they are believed to have settled near St. Joseph. No one knows the reason for this change because, strange to say, they have never written to their friends in Texas nor even answered letters sent them by members of our colony. Perhaps they learned in New Orleans of Grøgaard's death and then decided not to go to Texas.

II

The emigrants from Christiansand and vicinity who arrived in New Orleans in November, 1845, also abandoned the idea of going to Texas and went instead to Missouri with Annonsen, the master painter, and Lars Texe as leaders. They had an extremely difficult journey up the Mississippi, which at that season was full of ice. Only the Reiersen, Grøgaard, and Stiansen families went to Texas. The prospects of establishing a Norwegian colony in Texas were thus very dark. Grøgaard, therefore, settled in Nacogdoches, where he opened a small store with the money his wife had brought with her from Norway. [Gerhard] Reiersen, the watchmaker, and the carpenter, Stiansen, located there also. Christian Grøgaard died in 1846 at Grand Ecore on the Red River. He had fallen ill on his way home from

[23] Christian Reiersen and Andreas Ørbeck arrived with the second party from Norway.

New Orleans, where he had gone to buy merchandise. At almost the same time his two youngest children died. They had never been really well since their difficult North Sea crossing. A grown son passed away later. Of the three remaining sons, the twins are merchants, both well off, one [Hans J.] in Shreveport, one in Jefferson. The youngest is a farmer in Rusk County, married to a sister-in-law of his foster father, a rich American who brought him up after his mother's death early in 1848.

Thomas Grøgaard is also married to an American, but Hans Jacob [Grøgaard] married a daughter of Lassen Reiersen, who, with his brother Carl, had emigrated to Wisconsin.[24] Later both returned to Texas; the third brother, Andreas, still lives in Chicago. Three of Grøgaard's four daughters were grown when they left Norway. The oldest [Marie] lives in Prairieville; the second, Helene, married Georg Reiersen, also a brother of the editor. He is in business with his wife's brother and is a man of means. The third daughter was married to an American; she died, leaving a daughter. The youngest is married to an American doctor.[25] As Grøgaard had many friends and relatives in Norway, I thought the information about the fate of this family would be of interest, should your paper reach Norway, as I presume it will.

At the end of August, 1846, still another company of emigrants from Christiansand, under the guidance of Sexton [Ole] Reiersen, left for Havre de Grace. From there they took an American ship to New Orleans. There, several left the party to go to Wisconsin, while about fifty, chiefly natives of Omli Parish, continued their journey by steamer to Texas. But the low water in the [Red] river caused them to land at Alexandria. A Danish family, C. Lindberg (brother of the well-known scholar) with three children, and Mr. [James Hendrick] Staack from Lauenburg, continued up river by a smaller steamboat

---

[24] Hans Jacob Grøgaard, the younger, son of Christian, obviously was named for his illustrious Norwegian grandfather. (See *ante*, n. 19.) Grøgaard and Georg Reiersen operated a commission business in Shreveport.

[25] Mrs. Wærenskjold visited Christian Grøgaard's widow, Thomina, in Nacogdoches and was permitted to take the youngest daughter, Emma, to return and live with her. In 1857 Emma married Dr. Thomas Miller Matthews, a physician from a distinguished Virginia family. She is said to have been a dazzling beauty. Information furnished by Mr. Thomas Matthews, grandson of Dr. Matthews and Emma, and by Mrs. L. M. George, granddaughter of Carl Reiersen, both of Athens, Texas; Mrs. George to the editor, April 14, 1961. Andreas Reiersen was a ship's captain.

to Shreveport. [26] One of the Norwegians, Jørgen Olsen Hastvedt, who had become ill in Alexandria, was forced to stop at Milam, a small town in Texas, through which the Norwegians passed on their way inland. Several of the townspeople, notably a German merchant, gave this family, now in dire straits, all possible aid and assistance. Thus, when the town gave a barbecue on the anniversary [*March 2*] of Texan independence from Mexico, they supplied the Norwegians generously with different kinds of meat. And when the man died, everything for the funeral was provided, the women even sewing the shroud. Likewise, both men and women came to accompany the old man from distant Norway to his final resting place. Two hymns were sung before the casket was carried out, and they also sang hymns at the grave, where a pastor officiated. Everything was done in a solemn and fitting manner.

A few of this party stopped at Nacogdoches, while the majority went to Reiersen's, where they arrived on Christmas Eve. They settled, contrary to [J. R.] Reiersen's advice, in very unhealthful places. Thus, eight families crowded into two small rooms which an American had built in the bottom lands, completely surrounded by grainfields. The American, who knew how unhealthful it was, wouldn't live there himself but was glad to rent his undesirable place to the Norwegians. Three families also built themselves a cabin in the bottom lands, and one family went to the aforementioned Knud Olsen's. Lindberg and Staack, who had arrived a day earlier than the Norwegians, obtained a room at J. R. Reiersen's. All went fairly well until the warm season arrived; then almost everyone became ill, with the exception of J. R. Reiersen's family, whose house lay on high and healthful ground. Consequently many were discontented, and some had died when the writer of these lines arrived in the settlement

[26] The emigrant group of 1846 may have had the encouragement, rather than the active personal leadership, of Ole Reiersen, who had left Lillesand for Havre de Grace in March, 1845, and sailed to New Orleans that spring on the same ship with his son Johan Reinert and several other members of their immediate family. See earlier in this same letter. Mrs. C. E. Price of Clifton, Texas, relates how her mother, Marie Jensen, described J. R. Reiersen's manner toward arriving immigrant groups. "He was a big shot. He would sort the people just like cattle, pointing with a cane and saying, 'You go here. . . . You go there,' and so on." Then the newcomers had to work off the amount of their passage with the various neighbors who had put up the money for it. Interview with Mrs. Price, February 11, 1961. The scholar mentioned was probably Jakob Christian Lindberg (1797–1857), a famous Danish theologian, church historian, and orientalist.

in October, 1847. Nothing could be obtained to relieve the sick — no medicine, no doctor. Then Reiersen went down to Cherokee County to buy the most necessary medicine, and took the responsibility of doctoring the people himself, as he understood quite well how the common ailments of this region should be treated. There is little doubt that in this way he saved the lives of several people.

During the summer of 1847 a few more arrived from Norway, among them Torger Andersen from Mosseland Parish. He settled in Cherokee County, a few miles from the little town of Larissa, which was founded by Christian Reiersen and where several Norwegians settled later. After [Christian] Reiersen's death, however, all the Norwegians left Larissa; neither are there at present any Norwegians in Nacogdoches. The following winter Andersen went back for his family and also brought with him a couple of families from the Arendal region, who located in the nearby Brownsboro settlement, then called Normandy. These people came by ship directly from Arendal to New Orleans.

At the beginning of 1848 the foundation of a Norwegian settlement was laid at Four Mile Prairie in Van Zandt and Kaufman counties, about thirty-six miles from Brownsboro. As the name signifies, the prairie dominates the landscape, although there is no lack of woods, consisting exclusively of deciduous trees and some cedar. In its natural aspects this country closely resembles Denmark and is very pretty. Brownsboro, on the other hand, is more like Norway, as the land is very hilly and even has high ridges and large pine woods. It was really beautiful when the Norwegians first settled there. The forests were without underbrush, and there were a few small prairies of luxuriant grass, but these prairies were later overgrown with an almost impenetrable thicket, just as the bushes have shot up everywhere among the trees.

[J. R.] Reiersen was also the first Norwegian at Four Mile Prairie; he had bought a place there early in 1848, and in June of the same year Wilhelm Wærenskjold from Fredrikshald moved in, as well as the aforementioned Mr. Staack, and a Norwegian widow. The latter two had come to Texas the previous year. This was the region of the so-called Mercer's Colony, where every family that settled prior to

1849 obtained 640 acres, and a bachelor received 320 acres, paying $2 for the land certificate, plus the cost of the surveying.[27]

Meanwhile, the Norwegians in Brownsboro had regained their health, were contented, and had begun to realize what great advantages Texas had to offer the poor immigrant. Several had written glowing letters back to Norway. Consequently fourteen more families, mostly from Omli Parish, as well as several unmarried persons, arrived in the fall of 1850. Some located in Brownsboro, others at Four Mile Prairie. A few had come the same summer with Andreas Ørbeck, who had been on a visit to Norway. Ørbeck emigrated with Christian Reiersen and was the son of the late merchant Ørbeck, of Lillesand. Two members of his family accompanied him back, and later his stepfather, [Erick] Bache, the Lillesand merchant, and other relatives came. Among those who came with Ørbeck was a young man from Holt Parish, Terje Albertsen, who is now perhaps the richest Norwegian in Texas. He carries on a considerable business in partnership with his younger brother, Elef Albertsen, at Tyler, in Smith County. Elef Albertsen is especially well liked by everyone for his generosity and helpfulness.

In 1851, a couple of families came from Wisconsin, where they had settled in 1845. They were very discontented, remained only the one summer in Brownsboro without looking around further, and so returned to Wisconsin, where the fathers of both the wives lived. No doubt these two families were responsible for the cessation of emigration from the west of Norway, or more correctly Omli Parish, since that was their native district. In their letters they must have complained about everything in Texas, that land and conditions were definitely not so good as the older settlers had represented them.

[27] In the early days, much of Texas was settled by *empresarios* (private promoters). One of them, Charles Fenton Mercer, organized the "Texas Association," which, by a contract with President Sam Houston of January, 1844, was granted a large tract in north central Texas, including Van Zandt County. The area was given the name "Mercer Colony." The contract provided that Mercer receive ten sections of land for every hundred families brought into the district. Land speculators and squatters, eager to supplant the *empresario* arrangement with the Anglo-American land system, soon challenged the legality of the contract, and after much litigation it was declared invalid; however, the Texas legislature passed an act intended to safeguard the holdings of all those who were citizens of the colony as of October 25, 1848. Derwood Johnson to the editor, February 25, 1960; Walter Prescott Webb, ed., *The Texas Handbook*, 2:176 (Austin, 1952); Nancy E. Eagleton, "The Mercer Colony," in *Southwestern Historical Quarterly*, 39:275-291, 40:35-57, 114-144 (1935-37).

Among the immigrant arrivals in 1850 were a couple of old men from Hedmark, and in early 1852 a number of others also came from there, with a few from Holt Parish and Lillesand. Most of them settled in Four Mile Prairie, a few in Brownsboro, and [Erick] Bache, the merchant, went to Larissa, as his stepdaughter [*Ouline Ørbeck*], wife of Christian Reiersen, lived there. A few years after her first husband's death, this lady married J. R. Reiersen, who had become a widower in 1850 [*1851*]. After Christian Reiersen's death the Baches moved to Prairieville. In the spring of 1853, another party arrived, most of them from Hedmark but a few from the vicinity of Arendal.

With this group came [T.] Andreas Gjestvang, postmaster in Løiten, Hedmark, to inspect the country. No one ever found out what account Mr. Gjestvang gave of Texas upon his return; but this much is known — emigration from Hedmark to Texas stopped until two years ago. Then some Norwegians from Bosque went home to Norway and last year brought back more than a hundred immigrants; none of them went to eastern Texas, however.

Mr. Gjestvang, with a few Norwegians, made a trip to western Texas, and several of them decided to settle in Bosque County, which has attractive scenery, with valleys and limestone bluffs, but is not adequately supplied with woods. The region is well suited for raising wheat and is unquestionably very healthful, and thus from time to time Norwegians have moved from Brownsboro and Four Mile Prairie to Bosque, which is now a rather good-sized, flourishing settlement. (Many who first settled in Brownsboro moved from there to Four Mile Prairie and again from there to Bosque.) At present there are only seventeen Norwegian families at Four Mile Prairie, whereas three years ago there were thirty-four. Besides, there are a few widowers and a couple of young merchants, sons of J. R. Reiersen, who died in 1864. They live in the little town of Prairieville, founded by Reiersen, in that part of the settlement that lies in Kaufman County. One of them has a cotton gin, and Reiersen's widow has a wool-carding machine in partnership with a man named Pedersen from Hedmark.

J. R. Reiersen left four sons; the oldest [Oscar] is a lawyer and lives in Virginia, where he has married a lovable and rich young lady. The youngest is a clerk for one of his brothers. Reiersen's sister Lina was married to a rich German merchant and now lives in California.[28] [Erick] Bache's widow (he died in 1857 [*1867*]) owns the town's hotel, a considerable stock of horses and cattle, and a steam-driven sawmill in Anderson County managed by her brother, Andreas Anderson. There is also another sawmill in the same county, owned by Ole Jensen from Holt Parish. Several Norwegians are located in Anderson County, some of them very well situated; as, for instance, Søren Kolstad from Næs Foundry, who is postmaster, merchant, and watchmaker in Palestine [Texas].

In Brownsboro there are sixteen Norwegian families, and a few of these, especially Aslak Terjesen, are well off. They have considerable property, besides money out on loan. The settlement got its name from the little town, Brownsboro, founded by an American named Brown. A Norwegian merchant, [S.] Christian Halvorsen, from Næs Foundry once lived there, but he moved to Clifton in Bosque County. Reiersen, Wærenskjold, and [Ole] Gundersen from the vicinity of Christiansand established a steam-powered sawmill in Brownsboro on Aslak Terjesen's land in 1859; but the latter two soon sold out to John Hansen from Næs Foundry, and when the pinewoods were depleted, the mill was moved to another county. I will not say any more about the settlement at Bosque, because one of the oldest settlers there has promised to write a separate account of it. I merely want to mention that the capable machinist, Ole Knudsen — or, as he spells it, Canuteson — was one of the first to locate there and has contributed appreciably to the rise of the community by importing threshers and reapers, which he himself assembles.[29]

[28] Lina Reiersen married Mads[?] Vinzent, the storekeeper, who made a fortune speculating in Texas land, but was not aware of that fact until he had left for San Francisco, hoping to better his situation there. On their trip west the Vinzents were accompanied by Helen Reiersen, daughter of Carl. Virginia Carl Woods, granddaughter of Carl Reiersen, to Mrs. L. M. George, April 16, 1961. Eighteen years later Lina Vinzent returned to Texas for a visit. See letter of May 23, 1875, to follow.

[29] Ole Canuteson was born on the island of Karmøy near Stavanger, Norway, in 1832. He arrived in America with his parents in 1850. They went first to Illinois but, at the suggestion of Cleng Peerson, continued on to Texas, where they bought land ten miles south of Dallas. In 1853 they moved to Bosque County and became the founders of the large Norwegian settlement here. In 1868 Ole Canuteson moved to Waco, where he set up a foundry and machine shop. He was an intelligent and well-read man. See Anderson, *Norwegian Immigration*, 386–395.

It was in Bosque that old Cleng Peerson died, but he was also well known in eastern Texas. He often made long visits to the Reiersens and Wærenskjolds, where he was always a welcome guest. He had a great fondness for Texas, which he always considered the best of the states where Norwegians had settled. An old Norwegian by the name of [Johannes] Nordboe, who had first lived in the Northern states, settled in Dallas County long before the Reiersens came to Texas. Despite the fact that he had not seen any of his countrymen, other than his own family, for years, he had kept alive such a great interest in them that, though nearly eighty years old, he walked to Four Mile Prairie to visit the Reiersens and the Wærenskjolds. He was a man of means, but he was too weak to go on horseback and his sons, who did not share their father's interest in their countrymen, would not take him in a carriage. He was an interesting old man who had seen, read, and thought much.

There is a Swedish settlement in western Texas, but I know nothing about it. There are a few Danes in all of the Norwegian settlements but only one Swede, a Mr. Hallin, who lives in Prairieville and is married to Reiersen's sister [Gina]. She was first married to Andreas Ørbeck, who died in New Orleans in 1856.

It has been a serious drawback for the Norwegians in Texas that most of the time they have lacked a Norwegian-Lutheran pastor. They tried early to do something about this. At the suggestion of Wærenskjold the people in Four Mile Prairie agreed that they should write to Norway for a pastor. Early in 1855 the Reverend A. E. Fridrichsen arrived. He was also elected to serve as pastor in Brownsboro, but after three years he left for the North. After that we were without a minister until the Reverend O. Estrem came to Bosque in June of this year. He makes his home there but has promised to spend a couple of months of the year in each of the other settlements. He has held confirmation already in Bosque, and many of the confirmands were married people. In the short time that he and his wife have been here they have won the affection and respect of everyone. They themselves also say they are most content here, so we hope to keep them for many years.

In 1856 we had a visit from Elling Eielsen, whose brief activity in Texas deserves high praise. He promised to send us a minister, but when the war broke out all connections with the North were cut off, and, when the war was over, all normal work was crippled and everyone's resources were more or less limited. Very soon, however, the desire for a Norwegian pastor revived at Four Mile Prairie. Once again people gathered at Wærenskjolds' to consider the matter and after animated discussion agreed to appeal to the Norwegian Synod. This was Wærenskjold's proposal, while others preferred a preacher from the Eielsen group. In 1867 we were gladdened by a short visit made by Pastor Reque, but he could not fulfill our earnest wish to have the young people confirmed.[30]

As the majority of the readers of this magazine probably know no more about Texas than that it is the largest and southernmost state in the Union, I will add a few remarks concerning the country. The climate is mild, but far from as hot as one might expect from its southern location. It is seldom that the thermometer goes up to 100° F., while it is even more seldom that it drops below zero. The bitterest cold this writer has experienced in her twenty-two years in Texas was 4° below zero, and only once in that time did it rise to 112° F. Occasionally, however, it reaches 104° F., beyond which it rarely goes. One never hears of sunstroke here. The north wind can be very sharp and penetrating, but the cold lasts only a few days at a time — and even on Christmas Eve I have seen butterflies flitting about.

The soil is very fertile and yields all the northern and southern products, but cotton, corn, wheat, and sweet potatoes are the usual crops. Peaches are the commonest of the fruits, as the trees grow so easily from the pits and bear fruit the third or fourth year. Because of the mild climate and the sparse population one does not need to feed the domestic animals. They roam around at will, and consequently a man may own several hundred head of horses, cattle, sheep, or swine — yes, farther west, even several thousand. Some years ago it looked as if the grass would be entirely choked out by weeds, but two years ago God sent countless swarms of grasshoppers whose young, the following spring, destroyed the tender weeds, so the grass again took hold.

What one lacks most in Texas is labor. This is more noticeable

[30] Styrk Sjursen Reque (1836–1910), Norwegian Synod pastor and leader, came to America in 1845. In 1867 he was in Texas, temporarily serving a newly organized Norwegian church near Clifton, Bosque County, presumably at Norse.

now than before the war, which took away so many of our men. Many of the freed Negroes are lazy and do not care to exert themselves more than necessary to provide "plenty to eat," and that is easily done in Texas.

The state is a paradise for poor people, because anyone who will work can get a good job in any season and children are no burden, but a great help, to their parents. In the fall children can make good money picking cotton, which brings $.75 per 100 pounds, plus board. A good worker can pick 200 pounds a day, and, as it is light work, it can easily be done by children. Land is still very cheap but is rising in price. Anyone who cannot buy land can easily rent a field for half or two thirds of the yield, depending upon whether the owner or the renter supplies horses, equipment, and seed. All foodstuffs are inexpensive. A four-year-old steer costs $10, a sheep $1.50, fresh salt pork $.05 a pound, corn and sweet potatoes $.50 a bushel, and wheat $1. This year, however, wheat has gone up to $1.75 because the local crop was destroyed by grasshoppers last year. As a consequence of the difficulty of getting seed wheat, the crop this year is smaller than usual, because so much less was planted. A cow and calf, always sold together as the calf sucks the mother, who otherwise would not come home, cost $10.

I have no doubt that immigrants would do much better in going to Texas rather than to Minnesota. I am strengthened in this view because a Norwegian and a Dane, both of whom lived here awhile but now live in Minnesota, have written that they want to return to Texas this winter.

[ELISE WÆRENSKJOLD]

Vast Uninhabited Stretches[31]

PRAIRIEVILLE P.O.
KAUFMAN COUNTY, TEXAS
March 18, 1870

To THE EDITOR:

Please find enclosed the information you requested about the land available to the public in Texas. Mr. [Green J.] Clark is regarded as a competent lawyer and is the editor of the *Kaufman Star,* so I presume that his reports are completely reliable.

In the part of Texas where we live, all land has been claimed, so far as I know. The land which had not already been seized by land speculators was given to settlers many years ago — 640 acres to families and 320 acres to single persons. But vast stretches of land here (some of it very fine) are still uninhabited, as the owners live far away and have never shown themselves here during the twenty-one years that I have been living at Four Mile Prairie. If one went to a little trouble one could probably find out where they live, and acquire land from them. It is also possible to buy smaller tracts rather cheaply, partly improved, partly unimproved. A good and beautiful piece of land containing a small field and a little log house was recently sold in my neighborhood at $2 an acre.

We had a severe frost early this week, which crushed our hopes for a rich harvest of plums and peaches. The winter has been very hard, but this is the driest spring I have ever experienced in Texas. Last Tuesday morning the thermometer showed 20°, and I believe that is the coldest night we have had this winter.

Sincerely yours,
ELISE WÆRENSKJOLD

[31] This letter appeared on May 19, 1870, in the newspaper *Fædrelandet og emigranten* (La Crosse, Wisconsin). Under the vigorous leadership of Frederick Fleischer and F. A. Husher, this paper became one of the most influential conservative Norwegian-American publications. See Wist, *Festskrift,* chapters 1 and 2. Luther College has a microfilm file of *Fædrelandet og emigranten.*

Farming in Texas[32]

[To EMILIE SYVERTSEN:]

There is a difference between the two kinds of houses, however: in the first kind the boards are nailed on horizontally and in the second they are put up vertically. Both types of houses have to be paneled inside if they are to be any good. Anyone who has little or nothing to start out with had best build a log house, since he can improve that as he goes along. But he who can afford to buy lumber right away is wiser to build a frame or box house at once. I have a fairly large house (box) on the same place where a Norwegian-German family is now living. This family has rented one of my fields. One of my chimneys is built of stone and the other of brick, and I have a kitchen range and a stove. For these stoves we use only iron pipes that go up through the roof.

Most people also have smokehouses for the curing of meat and bacon, granaries, and stables for the horses; all these are built of oak logs. The stable is only for the horses you use every day or for horses of guests who may stay overnight. Many horses are never kept in the stable and never fed; they find their own food all the year round. I also have a kind of shelter for my sheep (completely open to the south and east) and a chicken coop; these, however, are an extravagance in Texas.

The courtyard is always fenced in either with rails or with some other kind of paling, and all the land you plan to cultivate is also fenced in with rails to prevent the cattle and hogs from getting in and ruining the crops. Rails are hewn from oak trunks that are cut into lengths of about eight or ten feet and are then split to the proper thickness with an iron wedge and a wooden club. Then the rails are placed across each other in this way, eight or nine rails high,

---

[32] The heading, salutation, opening, and conclusion of this letter are missing, but apparently it was directed to Emilie Syvertsen, as it was found in the Syvertsen collection. It was probably written, as were the other letters of 1870, to give information about Texas to the "in-laws" who were thinking of emigrating, and possibly was intended for publication in a newspaper. This may be the letter mentioned in the next one following, of May 1, 1870, as having been sent to Emilie "not long since."

and in each corner are placed two rails supporting each other with one rail on top of them.[33] A good rail splitter can make two hundred rails a day and is paid $.75 or $1 per hundred, plus board.

Wheat, rye, and barley may be sown from September to Christmas, but rye and barley are used only as green fodder for cattle in Texas, so they have to be sown in September. The crops planted then can be eaten off two or three times during the winter by the sheep, calves, and colts, and you can still get a good harvest for bread in June. But the Americans either plow the field up once more or harvest the crops for fodder.

Our ordinary potatoes are planted in January or February and may be eaten as early as April. They are grown only as food for the summer months, but they yield well. I weighed some potatoes that the maid brought in last summer and the biggest weighed one pound; three of them together, two and a half pounds. Sweet potatoes are grown in much larger quantities and are eaten during both summer and winter. The plant is very productive and the potatoes delicious. They are not boiled in water, but are baked in the oven.

Plowing preliminary to the corn and cotton planting can be done any time during the winter; the seeds are sown in rows about three feet apart. Corn is planted from the end of February until May, though early March is the best time. Cotton is sown from April 10 to May 10. When the plants have sprouted, a furrow is plowed at either side of them, and then the weeds and some of the cotton are hoed away. After this the whole middle area of the field is plowed once more and gone over again with the hoe; the field is then ready to be harvested. At the second hoeing all the corn and cotton in excess of the desired quantity is removed. The corn plant grows up with a tall stem having broad leaves and usually two ears. In August the leaves are picked off, dried, and used as fodder for the horses. During the plowing season the work horses are fed corn and fodder (leaves of corn), and sometimes oats too.

The cotton plant also grows quite tall, but it branches out more, like a tree, and has large yellow flowers that turn red before they are shed. On the same plant you may often see both yellow and red

---

[33] In the original there is a drawing here of rails laid in a crisscross design.

flowers. The cotton is picked when the ripe seed capsule opens, and the seed is then separated from the fibers in a cotton gin. You can pick cotton from August to Christmas; yes, even in January. It is easy work that pays well, from $.50 to $1.00 per hundred pounds; a person can pick from one hundred to as much as three hundred pounds a day, depending on the skill of the picker and the quality of the cotton. You can mow as much hay as you please out on the prairie, which is open to everybody. But the Americans do not want to take that trouble, and if you cannot mow the hay yourself, you are unable to hire anyone to do it for you. The Negroes say it is too hard work and they do not want anything to do with it.

You ask me if we have any milk cows here. Indeed we do — and many more than you have in Norway. But they do not yield as much milk as the Norwegian cows, since the calf, which sucks its mother until the cow herself weans it, gets half of it. Moreover, the cows practically starve during the winter months, and this reduces their yield a good deal. And it is not possible to develop a superior breed of cows, as all the cattle are left out together throughout the year. As the cows get calves, we drive them home to a pen. In the evening the cows return to the calves, and I then take one at a time into the pen to its calf. When the calf has sucked a little, I tie it with a rope to a pole and milk the cow (that is, half of the milk), and then I turn the calf loose. When all the cows have been milked, they are let into a larger pen alongside the first one, where the other cattle have been driven through another gate. Now the calves are let out to run where they please, but they return in the morning. When I have finished the morning milking, the cows are turned out on the prairie.

A good cow gives four to six quarts of milk; an average one, two quarts. During the winter you have to feed the cows and calves if you intend to milk, but most of them have to look after themselves — so they often die from starvation if the winter is severe. A cow and calf are worth from $10 to $15, depending on the quality. I have between fifty and sixty calves this year and expect more. I have also sold some cows this spring. All told, we have about three hundred head of cattle. They are marked in the ears and branded on the flank or shoulder, so that we can recognize them. A four-year-old ox is worth $10 or $12. The heifers get with calf when they are two or three years old.

Oxen are used for plowing and for pulling wagons; for the plowing between corn and cotton, we almost always use horses or mules, a hybrid of the donkey male and a mare. As a beast of burden the mule is regarded more highly than the horse. Horses and mules are broken, or, rather, they are trained to become riding and plowing animals, when they are two to five years old. Many people do not feed them at all when they are not being worked. Others feed their horses when there is little grass for them out on the plains.

Sheep are driven into a pen at night and let out again in the morning. As I have said, I have a shelter or house for them in the pen where they may seek protection during cold and rainy nights. When they get little ones, I let the lambs and the mothers browse in the rye field during the day.

[Elise Wærenskjold]

Land Prices Are Rising

Prairieville P.O.
Kaufman County, Texas
May 1, 1870

Dear Sister-in-Law [Emilie]:

Though it is not long since I wrote you, I feel that I ought to write a few lines and send you and your mother pictures of myself, Niels, and Tulli. Unfortunately they are not good, and it does not seem likely that I shall be able to get any good ones made. One of mine is a copy of a good portrait of me that was made at the same time as the one your mother got from Wilhelm. Otto would like very much to have that picture back when Grandmother dies. The other one I had taken in Tyler last year, but I did not want to send it because it is so bad. Still, I almost believe it is better than the copy. Do you not think that it would be possible to find your father's personal seal? Wilhelm often talked about this and was very sorry that his mother had lost it.

I had a letter from Elisabeth Wattner saying that they were embarking on the sixth of last month for New York. I hope they will arrive here in the fall; we will certainly do what we can to bring this about — if Wattner so wishes — but I will not make any attempt to talk them into coming here. My children sincerely wish that you would all come. Have you spoken to Amundsen? He has written to his friend here, Mr. Wilsen, that he plans to arrive in Texas sometime during the summer. I wish you would decide to come over in the fall. The letter from Mr. Svante Palm, the Norwegian-Swedish consul in Austin (the capital of Texas), which Wilsen sent to Amundsen, gives an absolutely correct description of conditions in Texas.[34] Land prices are rising, however, because of the good times, and many people have migrated to Texas from other states. Where vacant land (which belongs to the government) is available — and vast areas of this exist — every immigrant may obtain 160 acres if he is married and 80 acres if he is single — all this free of charge. In our immediate neighborhood there is no vacant land, however; but good land may be bought at $2 an acre. If there are buildings on the lot and the land has been tilled, the price is higher.

Nothing will come of Reiersen's trip. He probably realized that it would be too expensive to undertake. But if you want to come, you could probably find out in Christiania what would be the best way to get either to New Orleans or to Galveston, preferably to New Orleans. From that city you would have to go to Shreveport by steamboat, and there you would have to get in touch with the Norwegian firm of Reiersen and Grøgaard. I know both the owners of this firm; their bookkeeper, Sigurd Ørbeck, was one of your brother's best friends. Then you would go by railroad to Hallsville, one hundred miles from here, and there we could meet you in our wagon if you would let us know in time when you expect to be there. The fall is the best time to arrive in Texas. I am convinced that it would be wise for you to come; let me know — the sooner the better — what you decide to do.

[34] Svante Palm (1815–99), a journalist of independent views, was born in Småland, Sweden. He emigrated to Galveston, Texas, in 1844, and later settled in Austin, where he was appointed Norwegian-Swedish vice-consul. A highly cultured man, he is "best remembered for the large library which he accumulated during his long residence in Texas. These books, donated to the University of Texas, more than doubled the size of the University Library"; Webb, *Handbook of Texas*, 2:326.

Our pastor [*Estrem*] has been with us a month now; last Sunday Otto and Niels were confirmed, and last Wednesday we were received at the Holy Communion table. Thus my wish was granted: to see my children confirmed before I die.

Give our love to Grandmother and tell her that we are well. I cannot write to her this time because the letter is already too thick. I would like to know if she received the money I sent her three years ago. Ask her to write to me soon.

One more thing. Bring your own bedclothes with you if you come. The feathers used in feather beds cost $.75 per pound; thus a feather bed would run into some $20. Cotton cloth is cheap, $.12½ per yard (a yard is one and a half *alen*) for nice calico material; thus, clothes are not expensive. Good furniture is expensive and hard to get, but I imagine the cost of transportation would be too high if you were to bring your own from Norway. Yet I would bring at least a chest of drawers or a chiffonier. It is a good thing, however, that simple, every-day chairs cost only $1.25 apiece.

Well, now the paper is full, and I shall have to conclude with best greetings from Otto, Niels, and myself to all of you.

Your devoted

ELISE WÆRENSKJOLD

[*In the margin:*] If you should go to Galveston, get in touch with Even Jenson, who is working for B. R. Davids and Brothers.

Bring a Few Trees with You[35]

[PRAIRIEVILLE P.O.

KAUFMAN COUNTY, TEXAS

Summer, 1870?]

[DEAR EMILIE:]

You are probably surprised to hear from me so soon again, but as I am under the impression that you and your husband might sell your place and come over here in the fall (which I think would be

---

[25] The heading and salutation of this letter are missing. It is among those sent to Mrs. Wærenskjold's sister-in-law.

the best thing you could do), I thought I would call your attention to the fact that several people from Hedmark plan to come here in the fall. You can obtain all further information by writing to Jørgen Christophersen Spangen, Løiten, Hedmark. A foster daughter of Johan Dahl, the bookseller, has also written that she plans to come. The cheapest way would be to go by ship to Galveston or, preferably, to New Orleans, but in case this should not be possible, I have sent you a printed guide from which you may see what the cost would be from Hamburg to New Orleans. I must ask you to be good enough to send this guide to the said Jørgen Spangen. If you and your husband decide to come, then please write to Samuel Nicolai Hansen, the grocer in Lillesand, and let him know how he might send you a box of books for me. I have been waiting for these books since before the war, and this would be a good opportunity to get them here. Of course I shall be very grateful to you and happy to pay whatever expenses this box may cause you.

I should be very happy if you would bring a few trees with you. Of pear trees the following: empresses, bergamots, and gray pears. Of apples these: Gravensteins, glass apples, and pigeons. Of plums the following: green plums and St. Catherine plums; and some good cherry trees. Also bring some gooseberry and currant bushes. It goes without saying that I will pay for the trees and for their transportation here, and I will give you a good cow for your trouble. Speak to a gardener.[36] . . .

Brunswick cabbage yields fine heads here, and so does cauliflower. You probably think that I am a strange person to write all this when I do not even know for sure that you are coming. But if you are, it is best that you get this information in time. If you decide to come, the sooner you start the better, lest all the land hereabouts should be sold when you get here. Otto and Niels are very eager for you to arrive. Last Monday I almost bought a farm near Prairieville for you. But a man talked to the owner shortly after I had talked to him; this other person offered a little more than I did, so he got the farm. There was no risk involved in buying it, for if you did not come, I could easily have sold it to someone else and perhaps have made some money on it at that.

---

[36] One line in the body of the letter is missing, as the elision points indicate.

I must tell you a piece of news. On February 17, Otto became engaged to a very beautiful American girl of his own age. Her parents have been our neighbors as long as we have lived here. The wedding will probably be in the fall. It would be pleasant if Aunt and Uncle [Syvertsen] could be present for the occasion.[37]

Write soon and let me know if you plan to come and if you want us to buy a farm for you.

Now Otto is leaving for Prairieville, and therefore I must close with my best greetings to you, your husband, and your children from Otto, Niels, and your devoted sister-in-law,

ELISE WÆRENSKJOLD

Recently I sent a letter with some photographs. Greet Grandmother and tell her that we are well.

The Railroad Will Go Through

PRAIRIEVILLE P.O.
KAUFMAN COUNTY, TEXAS
May 24, 1871

DEAR SISTER-IN-LAW [*Emilie*]:

I was pleased to receive your letter of February 10 awhile ago, but I am sorry to hear that you have not sold your farm. It may, however, be all for the best, and perhaps you would not have been happy here. With 2,600 *spesiedaler* you could have made a good start, and the value of the land is rising, since it is expected that the southern railroad to California or the Pacific will go through our county not far from here.

I suppose you have received my last letter with Ophelia's picture for old Grandmother, but I imagine that she does not see very well any more. I have certainly got a beautiful, gracious, and pleasant daughter-

[37] Otto's bride was Ophelia Spikes, daughter of Israel Spikes, who was to be a witness at the trial of Dickerson in 1875. He was a committeeman in 1875 to help write the Texas constitution. Mrs. Dorsey Brown, Kaufman County (Texas) historian and a granddaughter of Israel Spikes, is quoted as saying that Spikes "was called the 'Big Swede' by his friends because he was arbitrator and peacemaker for the Norwegians and he had many friends among them." Mrs. Henry J. Gould to the editor, May 23, 1959.

in-law. Otto was married on March 2, and they are living with me until he can get a house built, which I hope will be sometime this summer. They plan to build a little to the north of my place. The wedding was held at the house of the bride's parents, of course, and was followed by a party in the evening. The following day we had a dinner at my house, and in the evening there was a dance to which a hundred and thirty persons were invited. We butchered two hogs, three turkeys, and twelve chickens. It does not cost as much to give a party in this country as in Norway, since people here usually do not use any other beverages than coffee, milk, and water. We do not have as many different courses either. At this dinner we had only roast, stew, several kinds of cake, and pie. What was left over from the dinner was served cold in the evening with coffee, and later that night we had coffee and cake for the third time. Everybody seemed to be having a good time.

I am very sorry to hear that poor old Grandmother is suffering want. If she only lived close to us she would lack neither food nor clothing. But it is difficult for me to save any money, as I have had so many expenses lately. I repaired my house and have to help Otto get a home built, and in addition to this I insured my life for $3,000 and sent the Wattners $150 to cover their traveling expenses to this country. Thus you can understand that my expenditures have been great. I am now expecting your sister and Wattner every day, as they wrote that they would be leaving New York in April. I have received several letters from them since they arrived in New York. Elisabeth and little Carl have been ill a good deal of the time, but when they wrote last month they were all well. If you want to write to Elisabeth, send your letter to me. Wattner is in debt in New York; probably his income there was quite small. But if he comes here and is sensible and industrious, I am sure that he will be able to pay all of it in time. It grieves me, though, to hear about Grandmother's money; she should not have lost it that way.

We now have lots of ripe plums and cherries, and people come every day to eat our plums. In earlier days few around here planted fruit trees, but all kinds of fruit trees are now becoming fairly common.

With much love to you, your husband and children, and also to

Grandmother, from Otto, Ophelia, Niels, and myself, I remain your devoted

ELISE WÆRENSKJOLD

P.S. Be so good as to put the enclosed letter in an envelope and address it to Captain Christopher Taarvig, Fredrikstad, and mail it for me, too, please. Let me know if my brother-in-law [*Oscar Syvertsen*] has completely given up the idea of coming to Texas.

Otto Was Married

PRAIRIEVILLE P.O.
KAUFMAN COUNTY, TEXAS
May 27, 1871

TO MRS. THOMINE DANNEVIG:

Otto was married the second of March to Ophelia Florence Spikes, a beautiful girl, both kind and able, who is three months younger than he. It was a candlelight ceremony in the evening and, of course, took place at her home. The next day we had the wedding dinner, followed by a dance in the evening at our house, to which one hundred and thirty guests — some American and some Norwegian — were invited.

Otto and Ophelia are not setting up housekeeping, but are living with me for the present. As soon as possible a house will be built for them, a little north of mine; I think they will be able to move in by Christmas. You are surprised, no doubt, that Otto is married, and you will be no less surprised to hear that Mother Bache on April 13 ceased to be Mother Bache — she married a German widower, Oscar Pabst. He has two nice little girls, five and nine years old, and is said to be rich. Mother Pabst lives very well, has much property and a good income from a hotel, sawmill, farm, horses, cattle, etc. It was a small wedding but beautifully arranged. The following Sunday, Norwegian services and baptism were held at my house. The newly-weds, Pastor Estrem, and all those present remained here for dinner.

You must excuse me if this letter is not as it should be, but as I write I am watching a kettle of cherries, which I am canning. We have some cherries and lots of plums, which are ripe now, and so many people, black and white, acquaintances and strangers, come for plums.

As for the Franco-Prussian War, we have read more than enough about it in the papers. I understand the Norwegians have been in complete sympathy with the French, but what do they say now? The war is over and still the Frenchmen have not had enough of misery and bloodshed. To be sure, I would rather have seen the French win than the all-devouring Prussians, but the fact is that I do not like either of them. We have read about the balloon and the bazaar in Christiania.[38]

[ELISE WÆRENSKJOLD]

Many Expenses and Little Income

PRAIRIEVILLE P.O.
KAUFMAN COUNTY
May 12, 1873

To MRS. THOMINE DANNEVIG:

I have a good deal of property, to be sure, but also many expenses and little income. Last winter was especially difficult for all those who have livestock. In the first place, the last part of the summer and the entire autumn were so dry that the animals became very thin, because the grass had withered. In the second place, winter came early and was extremely cold, and at Christmastime all the horses were hit by a disease that had spread over the whole United States. All these things taken together caused the death of horses, cattle, sheep, and hogs, even though we used a great deal of grain besides our hay, trying to keep them alive. My loss through the death of animals and the extra grain consumed amounted to more than

[38] James C. M. Hanson, Norwegian-American librarian, states in his unpublished memoirs that "when a French balloon, with two officers aboard, which had escaped from Paris, then encircled by German troops, landed in the mountains to the southwest of us [North Aurdal, Valdres], a great bazaar was organized in our little community for their benefit." Hanson, "What Became of Jens," a manuscript record filed in the Koren Library, Luther College, Decorah, Iowa. The bazaar referred to by Mrs. Wærenskjold was undoubtedly occasioned by the same balloon flight.

$200, not counting what Otto and Niels lost. It has naturally cost me a good deal, too, helping Otto get started.

Last winter I had a visit from a son [Tony Meldahl] of my cousin [Emil,] (a son of Mother's youngest brother), in West Virginia, and his cousin from Sweden. They were two handsome, refined young men, and it was an unexpected pleasure for me to have a relative in my home.

[ELISE WÆRENSKJOLD]

A Mild Punishment

PRAIRIEVILLE P.O.
KAUFMAN COUNTY, TEXAS
March 6, 1875

DEAR MADAM STAACK:

Many thanks for your friendly letter. It pains me very much that you are neither in good spirits nor in good health — the former I could, of course, well imagine. It must be very unpleasant for you not to be able to be with Hans when he is sick. How far away is he? I hope that he is better now.[39] It was good news indeed that you got from Norway. I too have heard recently from the people at Næs Foundry; namely, from Marie Thomsen.

I hope we are finally finished with the Dickerson case. He was condemned to ten years' imprisonment by the last session of the court — a mild punishment, to be sure, for such a cold-blooded and long-premeditated murder. His lawyer, [George W.] Chilton of Tyler, appealed to the supreme court, however, so we may still have some more trouble with it. We have been in Kaufman six times in this connection and are to pay the lawyers $250.[40] Furthermore, Otto lost

[39] Hans Jenson was Madam Staack's son by her former marriage to Jens Jenson.
[40] N. T. Dickerson was the man who killed Wilhelm Wærenskjold. For a discussion of the case, see the introduction to this volume. The legend is that one of the Reiersens "became constable after Wilhelm's murder and that he found Dickerson plowing in a field and brought him back to Kaufman for trial — and then there were no witnesses"; Mrs. Gould to the editor, April 6, 1959. Derwood Johnson, who is an attorney, writes, "In Texas there are no statutes of limitation in connection with prosecutions for murder and treason. . . . The 'Special Prosecutor' is usually employed and paid by family and/or friends of the deceased in a murder case," the

a very good mare the first time we were in Kaufman, so it has cost us a lot. The last time, we were there a whole week. After that I had to go to court in Canton about our land; but nothing could be done, since John S. Martens, the man we bought the land from, did not show up. I stayed there four days, all to no avail.

Niels, Oscar Andersen (who works for Niels), and Rosell, the French tailor who traveled around here seven or eight years ago as a peddler and who now rooms at Niels's, keep up such a talkfest that I hardly know what I am writing. Beruld Olsen and Juliane live at the parsonage and Juliane keeps house for Niels. Olsen helps him in the field, and, besides, he has a Negro, Cloburn; but then, he has a lot of land. He leased about twenty-two acres from me, and also he acquired eighteen acres of new land on his own account. Niels is up every morning now before dawn and lights the fires. It is a great change from earlier days when I could hardly get him up when breakfast was ready.

I sowed eight acres to rye last fall, but the seed must have been damaged, because hardly anything came up — a great loss to me, for I could not bring the sheep in [from pasture] when they were to lamb, and consequently many died. Yesterday we had beautiful warm weather, and if it had only lasted a day longer I would have finished sowing the oats for Niels and myself — what is ready for sowing — but today it is snowing, so the ground will soon be entirely white. This is the first snow of the year, but we have had unusually steady cold and more cloudy weather than I remember here in Texas.

I wrote to Berte Wilsen today, and if you read each other's letters you will get a fuller account. From her letter you will see that I now have two granddaughters [Florence and Lilli].

Otto, Niels, and I greet you and all your children most kindly. May I also ask you to greet all my acquaintances in Bosque whom you may happen to speak with? Here is the end of the paper and I must quit. I hope you will get along well and that you will write to your

ELISE WÆRENSKJOLD

P.S. I keep house by myself.

purpose of this arrangement being to let "the jury know that . . . the family wants a conviction of the murderer." Derwood Johnson to the editor, November 30, 1960.

Visitors from California

[PRAIRIEVILLE P.O.]
May 23, 1875

To Mrs. Thomine Dannevig:

Here we live in the same old way and as usual enjoy good health. Otto's wife and youngest child, Florence Maud, were both baptized two weeks ago today by a Methodist minister. Ophelia's parents are Methodists, but she would have been willing to be baptized by our pastor [Estrem] if he had not demanded that she learn the catechism by heart.[41]

My two grandchildren are pretty youngsters. Lilli [Lillian Leota] is very lively and impetuous, while Florence is very patient.

Day before yesterday I was invited to a party at Johan Reiersen's, with Mother Vinzent [Lina Reiersen] and her daughter, visitors from California. After an absence of eighteen years, she has come this long way to see her relatives once more.[42]

I understand that you have been to Tønsberg. Did you see Foyn? I have often read in the newspapers about his successful whaling.

[ELISE WÆRENSKJOLD]

[41] Otto and Ophelia had eleven children, of whom only three lived to adulthood: William, Ethel, and Lillian Leota. Ophelia died in 1900 and Otto later married Ovie Spikes, widow of his wife's brother John. Their son, Otto Mackey Warenskjold of Cleburne, Texas, is the owner of four water colors that originally belonged to Elise, one of them done by her. Lillian Leota Wærenskjold married James Aaron Feagin, who now lives in Fort Worth, Texas; Mrs. Henry J. Gould is his daughter. Mrs. Gould to the editor, January 6, 1961; Henry J. Gould to the editor, January 23, 1961.
[42] Johan (John) Reiersen, was the son of Johan Reinert.

Lights and Shadows
on the Prairie

1876–1889

I Milk the Cows

PRAIRIEVILLE P. O.
KAUFMAN COUNTY, TEXAS
June 11, 1876

DEAR SISTER-IN-LAW [*Emilie*]:

It is now a long time since we heard from you; I do not know where you live, but Wattner thinks that you will receive this at the old address.

Your sister [*Elisabeth Wattner*] has had a sweet little boy since I wrote you last — his name is Hans Arne Emil; but I pity her, for she has had a hard time of it, suffering badly from asthma this spring. She is fairly well now, however. Thorvald has grown up to be a nice boy and is a great help to his mother.

Wattner has fenced and cultivated some of his land; this year he will have a little rye and wheat and some cotton. They also have potatoes and vegetables and quite a few young fruit trees. He got $250 from his uncle, Mr. Christensen, which was a great help to him. Betha was so happy that she cried for joy when they received the bill of exchange.[1]

I have a young widow staying with me, a daughter of one of my mother's brothers. She had a baby boy last winter, and he and your sister's little son were baptized on the same day in our small new church. All the godparents had dinner at my house. Wattner and Betha were the godparents of Therese's little son.

[1] Betha is an abbreviation for Otilde Fredrikke Elisabeth (Mrs. Adolph S. Wattner), Wilhelm's sister.

109

Niels and I share the household expenses, and Therese takes care of the cooking and general housekeeping. I milk the cows and tend the garden. I have planted a patch of potatoes and sweet potatoes, and look after that myself. Our ordinary potatoes are now ready to be dug, but you do not dig sweet potatoes until there is danger of frost. We have already harvested our barley, rye, and wheat.

Otto and his wife and child are well; they expect an addition to the family soon. If they had been allowed to keep the other dear children, they would have quite a little flock. Lilli is a very lively girl, wilder than any of my children have ever been.[2]

Do write soon now and let me know your address and how you and your family are.

My children and the Wattners send their best greetings.

Your devoted sister-in-law,

ELISE WÆRENSKJOLD

We Have a Church

PRAIRIEVILLE P.O.
KAUFMAN COUNTY, TEXAS
October 22, 1876

DEAR EMILIE:

I received your kind letter of July 22 some time ago and was happy to hear that you are all well. Of course poor Oscar [Syvertsen] must have had a bad time with his leg, but I suppose that he is completely recovered now. Fanny certainly became engaged at an early age. I am happy to hear that she is making a prosperous match, and I wish her much good fortune and happiness.[3]

Otto's baby girl was born on August 4 [3] and was named Louise Elizabeth. The first name is for Ophelia's mother [*Mrs. Israel Spikes*]; the second for me, my mother [*Elisabeth M. Tvede*], your sister [*Elisabeth W. Wattner*], and a sister of Ophelia's father. We

---

[2] The expected child, Louise Elisabeth, was born August 3, 1876, and lived less than a year. Otto and Ophelia had lost two infant children earlier. Lilli (Lillian Leota) lived until 1921.

[3] Fanny was Emilie and Oscar Syvertsen's daughter. She married John Skjolden.

are all well except Lilli, Otto's little girl, who has suffered attacks of ague every other afternoon.

Poor Betha! She has had a very bad summer, as she has suffered from asthma, and little Hans has had scrofula. Betha has not been in my house since last spring, when little Hans was baptized.[4] Wattner is still much in debt, for he broke a large field and bought a wagon and two mules. In the beginning, when you clear a new field, expenses are, of course, heavy and income small; and though victuals and clothing are cheap, it takes quite a bit to support a family of six. Betha will write to you when she gets more time. Thorvald is now able to help her quite well with many things, but these days she and Carl have to pick cotton. Wattner believes that he will get about a thousand pounds of cotton, but unfortunately prices are low this year. Since the beginning of August we have not had one good rain, so the grass is quite dry. Many of the water tanks were empty, but yesterday we had a little rain and there is water in the tanks again. This has been the shortest summer I can remember since I came to this country. We had frost on May 3 and again on October 1.

I suppose we shall lose our pastor [Estrem] soon, as he wants to move to Minnesota; but he will not leave until we have another one. We do not know yet who the new minister will be. I do not remember if I told you that we have a church now. Earlier, divine service was held in my house.[5]

Recently two Norwegians arrived from Michigan. They are going to rent land very soon, and if they like it here many others will come also, about a hundred, it is believed. If this happens, then we in Prairieville and Brownsboro congregations can get a pastor of our own, which would be a much better arrangement. Brownsboro is only a day's journey from here, while Bosque, where the pastor now lives, is a hundred and twenty miles away.

Now, dear Emilie, I shall conclude, with much love from my children and myself to you and your family. Write to me soon. Your devoted

ELISE WÆRENSKJOLD

[4] The Wattners had had five children, one of whom died in Norway. The others were Thorvald, Carl, Fredrik, and Hans.
[5] A new church was built at Four Mile in 1875.

Our Settlement Is Small[6]

PRAIRIEVILLE P.O.
KAUFMAN COUNTY, TEXAS
November 10, 1876

Dear MADAM QUÆSTAD:

Excuse me for taking the liberty of asking you if you would be willing to contribute one dollar toward getting a board fence around the graveyard where your mother is buried. You know that our settlement is small and many of us are widows. I therefore hope that those of our friends in Bosque who have relatives buried here will not think harshly of me for making this request. If there is anything amiss in so doing, the fault is mine alone. If, out of your goodness, you are willing to contribute something, you may send it in an ordinary letter.

You, your husband and daughter, and the Ringnæses are greeted most kindly from your friend,

ELISE WÆRENSKJOLD

We Share Our Letters

PRAIRIEVILLE P.O.
KAUFMAN COUNTY, TEXAS
August 31, 1877

To MRS THOMINE DANNEVIG:

I received your very welcome letter on July 31 just after I had accompanied my children (Otto and his family) a part of the way on their trip to northwest Texas. I read it with much interest, and several days later I walked over to Ouline Reiersen's and read it to her and to her brother [Sigurd Ørbeck]. We folks from Lillesand always share our letters from home, and when we get one like yours, it is really a special occasion for us.

---

[6] A photostatic copy of this letter was furnished by Derwood Johnson from an original in the possession of Mrs. Ole J. Hoel.

This year our cotton yield will be unusually poor, scarcely one fifth of what we would get under normally good conditions. My sons planted a lot of cotton because that is the crop most likely to bring in money. We had too much rain in the spring and too little during the summer.

Otto wants very much to move farther west, because many seem to think that the land there is more fertile and the climate more healthful. But as for me, in my old age, it is not at all pleasant to think of starting over again with all the uncertainties of pioneer life.

Otto and his family came back on Monday, having been away four weeks. They traveled several hundred miles, and the total cost of the trip was $6. This will no doubt seem unbelievable to you, but they took provisions and bedding along from home, cooked their own meals, and slept in the wagon. This is not unusual in Texas.

[ELISE WÆRENSKJOLD]

Texas Should Be Praised [7]

PRAIRIEVILLE P.O.
KAUFMAN COUNTY, TEXAS
December 29, 1878

[TO THE EDITOR:]

I see that a certain Mr. Larsen reports to your paper that "the Norwegian settlements in Texas have dwindled so much that within a not very remote future there will probably not be a trace of them left." I should like to say that Mr. Larsen must be badly informed, especially when he states, as the reason, that the Norwegians are not able to acclimatize themselves to Texas. The good man could easily convince himself of the opposite if he would visit the Norwe-

[7] This letter appeared January 8, 1879, in *Norden*, a leading Norwegian-American weekly published in Chicago, 1874–97. Among *Norden*'s editors were such well-known figures as Halvard Hande, Thrond Bothne, and Peer Strømme. It has been characterized as "the most literary of Norwegian immigrant papers." It was Democratic at a time when most Norwegian Americans were Republicans, a fact that may help to explain its demise. See Wist, *Festskrift*, 85–87. Luther College has a microfilm file of *Norden*.

gian colony in Bosque County. I am living in the Norwegian settlement at Four Mile Prairie in the eastern part of Texas — and have been living here for more than thirty years, and I can truthfully say that my health has been as good as I could expect it to be in only the most wholesome places on our earth. Yet I must admit that the western part of Texas is more healthful than the eastern, and this is the main reason why several families have moved from here to Bosque. Other reasons are that the soil is more fertile and that the Norwegian pastor lives in that settlement. There can be no doubt that the number of Norwegians in Texas, far from decreasing, is increasing with every year.

Our new pastor arrived in Bosque last fall, but has not honored us with a visit yet, even though his letter of call stipulates that he spend three weeks in our settlement every autumn and spring and the same period of time in Brownsboro. This does not look very promising for us.[8]

We had a fairly good harvest this year; nevertheless, the times are very hard, for the prices of agricultural products are lower than they have ever been. Besides, we have had the driest autumn I can recall; consequently, it was very late before people could sow their wheat. And no sooner had the wheat sprouted, shortly before Christmas, when we had a severe frost, so I fear the crop has been ruined. Many of these mornings the thermometer has been at 20°. Well, probably the good people in the North think this is nothing, as I imagine the temperature up there often gets below zero. Since I came to Texas we have had such a low temperature only once before.

We had a good deal of illness in the community last summer, but there was only one death among us Norwegians. The one who died was an old woman, Marie Grøgaard, a granddaughter of M. J. [H. J.] Grøgaard, the author of the reader for children.

I have heard that there are plans to found one or two new Norwegian settlements still farther west than Bosque. I do not know

[8] The new pastor was John Knudsen Rystad, 1848–1932. He served various Texas congregations, 1878–1925, and was chairman of the Clifton (Texas) College Corporation, 1897–1905. Mrs. Rystad (Berghitte Gunhild Nelson), who was born at Prairieville in 1859, was baptized by Elling Eielsen. She is said to have been a devoted worker for her husband's widespread and demanding pioneer parishes. "When the saga of the Protestant pastor's wife is told, it will be discovered that she possessed in superlative degree all of the virtues of her kind"; *Lutheran Herald* (Minneapolis), March 20, 1934.

anything definite about this; but if anyone wants to come to Texas, I would advise him to go to the western part of the state.

In conclusion I merely wish to add that never, either directly or indirectly, have I profited in the slightest way by praising Texas. I have praised Texas because I found that she should be praised.

ELISE WÆRENSKJOLD

I Have to Feed My Cattle

PRAIRIEVILLE P.O.
February 24, 1882

To MRS. THOMINE DANNEVIG:

I would very much like to visit Otto and his family [in Hamilton County], for they have a little girl who was born February 11, but such a journey would cost at least $15, and that I cannot afford.[9] Then, too, I have to feed my cattle every morning and my sheep every evening, and they cannot be neglected. On January 1, I had fifty-eight sheep and fifty-eight cattle, but now I have sold fourteen of the latter and have acquired a number of lambs. Since January 5 it has rained so much and so often that most of the time we have had to walk around in deep mud inside the enclosures where we feed the stock.

Today the ground had dried enough so that I was able to plant cabbages, onions, and tomatoes, but now it is raining again. I take orders for seed for James Vick in New York, thereby earning a few dollars, besides paying for the garden seed for myself and my children. But to get the orders I have to walk many a mile, since I have no horse.

During Christmas we had the most delightful weather that anyone could wish for. I understand that Norway is also having an unusually mild winter.

Niels and I are still living in the same house, but I do my own housekeeping. This doesn't amount to much, as my food consists almost exclusively of tea and bread. Niels has a very sweet and beau-

_____

[9] The little girl was Ethel Murilla Wærenskjold. She married Walter Bailey.

tiful little boy; his little girl is frightfully spoiled.[10] Otto now has three children living—four of his children have died. He and his family visited us this summer, and it was a great pleasure for me, although they spent most of the time with her [*Ophelia's*] family, as she has many relatives here.

[ELISE WÆRENSKJOLD]

Ruined by Doctors and Lawyers

PRAIRIEVILLE P.O.
November 10, 1882

To MRS. THOMINE DANNEVIG:

This summer I visited my dear Otto again and some old friends in Bosque. I traveled both ways by train, and since the fare has been lowered to $.03 a mile, the whole trip cost a little over $9. They have built a plain little house in a very beautiful spot with a charming view, and their sheep, which are their means of livelihood, did well last winter.[11]

Otto wanted me to move out to his place in Hamilton County, and I had planned to do so next summer, but that is not God's will. Shortly after I left, a disease broke out among the sheep; Otto became afraid and decided to sell his flock, and presumably the land and house also, and to move to the town of Hamilton to open a small business. Thus there was no longer any occasion for me to think about moving. As long as my health is good, things go well, and it does not help to worry about the morrow. I hope that God will arrange everything well for us.

Here we are ruined by doctors and lawyers. The former very seldom receive much from me, but my children, on the other hand,

[10] Niels Wærenskjold married Florida Eliza Pate ("Babe") May 5, 1878; they were divorced April 20, 1895. They had nine children, one of whom died in infancy. Some of their descendants have changed their name to Van Shaw; Mrs. Gould to the editor, January 6, 1961. The children Elise mentions were Calvin and Fannie.

[11] Halvard Hande, editor of *Norden*, was in Texas during the summer of 1882 and sent several reports back to his paper. In one of August 30 is this note: "In Bosque I had the pleasure of meeting Mrs. Wærenskjold, who was passing through from eastern Texas to visit a son in Hamilton County and was kind enough to look me up. She is an especially lively and interesting old lady."

have to "shell out" liberally to them. The lawyers, however, are to blame for my being poor.

Another bad thing for the farmer is that he cannot hire help except at such unreasonable wages that it doesn't pay. Therefore one must either rent out the farm or let the land lie fallow. Usually we must provide the renter not only with a house but also with work animals, machinery, and food for him and his animals; yes, and often clothing as well. If a renter is not industrious and honest, he leaves while still in debt to the owner for a small or large amount. Very often, when the time comes to pick the cotton, the renter says he is so much in arrears that he needs the whole crop to pay it. Then, if he is dishonest, he goes his way and picks cotton for another man to whom he is not indebted. Thus it went with Niels last year, and thus it goes this year also. One renter last year left with a debt of $75, another with one of $50. This year a family moved away owing $50 and another owing even more.

[ELISE WÆRENSKJOLD]

I Read Everything about Norway

PRAIRIEVILLE
September 23, 1883

To Mrs. THOMINE DANNEVIG:

I have read Husher's travel letters with the greatest interest, but it grieves me to see that politics in Norway have generated so much bitterness and hatred. It seems very natural to me that in both politics and religion people can have different opinions, but to hate one another because of them seems very unchristian. As I may have told you, Husher kindly sends me his paper free of charge, and so does Relling, the publisher. I always read everything about Norway, while I skip everything about the elections in the Northern states and the religious controversies in the Lutheran Church in America.[12]

---

[12] F. A. Husher was publisher of *Fædrelandet og emigranten*, and I. T. Relling, of *Norden* (see part 2, note 31, and part 3, note 7). In both America and Norway, politics were vehement and personal in those days. The presidential elections of 1880 and 1884 in the United States, for instance, were notoriously vicious. In the Northern states,

Greet Thorvald for me and ask him if he will be kind enough to send me Jonas Lie's *Livsslaven*. Your son Niels [*Nils*] once sent me *Et dukkehjem*, and Lerche, a book which his painter son wrote. It interests me so much to see something from our recent authors, but I cannot afford to buy them. I certainly thank God, however, that I am in good health and have my daily bread.[13]

I left home June 30 and ate dinner at Mother Pabst's in Wills Point, our nearest railroad station, fifteen miles away. Toward evening I continued by train to Clifton, a distance of one hundred and fifty-seven miles, where I arrived the next morning in time for breakfast. It would not take more than seven hours except that one must change trains halfway and wait several hours during the night in the depot, which is most tiresome.

Clifton lies in the large Norwegian settlement of Bosque County. As the railroad does not go nearer Hamilton than Hico, twenty miles away, I decided to go to Clifton. I have many friends and acquaintances among the Scandinavians there, so it did not cost me anything to reach Otto's. I arrived the first of July to find both him and his wife ill, which was very distressing, the more so as Otto had written that he was well. But they soon improved enough so that he could attend to his business and she to her house. While I was there, they also had a visit from her mother [*Mrs. Spikes*], two of her unmarried brothers, her oldest brother with his wife and four children, and her oldest sister. So at one time we were sixteen persons in the house. I stayed a month, and then Otto brought me to the Norwegian settlement [*Norse?*], where I also spent a month

these were also the years when politicians "waved the bloody shirt" and "twisted the lion's tail" to arouse political fervor by impassioned allusions to the Civil War and the actions of Great Britain. In Norway during 1872–85 the Conservative and Liberal parties were formed as a result of disputes over the royal veto and the parliamentary system of government. The Norwegian-American Lutheran denominations were at this time convulsed by debates about predestination.

[13] Jonas Lie (1833–1908) was one of Norway's greatest novelists. His *Livsslaven* (One of Life's Slaves — 1883) was one of the first naturalistic works in Norwegian literature. Ibsen's *Et dukkehjem* (A Doll's House) seemed very revolutionary in 1879, when it was written. Nora, the main character, left home because she discovered that she was a mere plaything in a male-dominated society. Vincent Stoltenberg Lerche (1837–92) was a minor Norwegian painter. The book that Mrs. Wærenskjold refers to was probably *Med blyanten* (With the Pencil), published in 1873–74, a collection of illustrated travel sketches and essays. Further information about Norwegian authors mentioned in this volume can be found in any standard history of the subject. See, for example, Harald Beyer, *History of Norwegian Literature* (New York, 1956), or Theodore Jorgenson, *History of Norwegian Literature* (New York, 1933).

visiting around from one to the other of my acquaintances, and had a very enjoyable trip.

In Bosque you do not know anyone except [the younger] Andreas Anderson, the son of Mother Pabst's brother. Naturally I visited there also. He has a friendly, capable wife and a great many children. Bosque celebrated the Seventeenth of May with a festival dinner and speeches. The Norwegian minister [*John K. Rystad*] gave a talk in Norwegian, while a Norwegian professor named Anderson from Austin (the capital of Texas) gave a talk in English. Both were said to have been very good.[14]

[ELISE WÆRENSKJOLD]

He Liked Texas [15]

[PRAIRIEVILLE]
March 31, 1884

DEAR MARIE:

No doubt you have wondered why I did not answer your very welcome letter sooner. The reason is that my husband's sister [*Elisabeth Wattner*] and her three sons have been sick since the middle of February. She and the oldest son [*Thorvald*] are still in bed but are now out of danger. There were two weeks, however, when it seemed more like death than life for them. Niels has also been in bed from time to time, and his wife stayed in bed four days. Finally, I also had a mild attack of chills and fever but recovered quickly without the aid of a doctor.

It was very sad that Petrine had to die so early. I had no idea, when I was in Bosque, that it was to be the last time I should see her and her mother-in-law. I can greet you from the [Aanon] Knudsens. I saw Tulla today and they are all well. Julie Knudsen, Aan-

[14] John J. Anderson (1840?–96) was born in Norway and was educated at Beloit College. About 1880 he became professor and business manager at Tillotson Institute in Austin, Texas. Halvard Hande reported in *Norden*, March 11, 1883, that Anderson and an English architect had set up a business college in Austin.

[15] Ten letters and one post card from Mrs. Wærenskjold to Marie Staack (Mrs. Stephen A. Jensen), have been presented to the Norwegian-American Historical Association by Mrs. C. E. Price of Clifton, Texas, daughter of Mrs. Jensen.

on's oldest daughter, was recently married to an American widower who owns nothing; otherwise I do not know anything about him.[16] He is a renter and has lived in Schofstad's old house, so I suppose Julie had a good opportunity to learn to know him. A Dane has come to Prairieville; he has gone into a kind of partnership with Oscar Mjaaland in saddle making.

I do not know whether you remember the Kuckerells, but your mother [*Madam Staack*] undoubtedly does. The man who bought Knud Hansen's place fell out with his neighbor — an old man whose name, I believe, was Hart — and shot him three times. The man is not dead, but I do not know if he will live. It is terrible that such things happen and that they happen so often. However, Texas is not so horrible a land as Mr. Untervald [*Underthun*] pictures it in *Norden*. I have been expecting that someone in Bosque would answer him, but as yet I have seen nothing from there except a little piece by B. Olsen of Tyler. I think it is quite brazen thus to slander everything and everybody.[17]

How is your old mother getting along? Greet her very warmly for me. Is Ericksen still with you? How are Ragnhild and old Wilsen, now that the Wilsens have left them? I have still not received a letter from Berta, even though I have written to her twice. Hoff has been at Otto's, and he told them that Wilsen had died; but Mrs. Spikes says it is not so. You may not have heard that Done Spikes is married to Standley, a farmer, and Fanny to an Adventist. I believe his name is McCutchen or something like that.

Last fall we had a visit from an engineer, Nils Wærenskjold, an exceptionally fine and pleasant man who had spent half a year in

[16] Aanon and Tulla Knudsen's farm adjoined that of the Wærenskjolds. Their daughter is mentioned later as Julie Small.

[17] Mrs. Wærenskjold mistakenly wrote "Untervald" for "Underthun." Andreas Larsen Underthun was a theological student who left Luther Seminary for Texas early in 1883 in hopes of bettering his health. He secured a teaching position in a Swedish settlement near Round Rock. In *Norden* of February 12, 1884, he published a rather facetious letter sharply censuring Texas and the "old Texans." His estimate of immigrants from Europe was more charitable; they were law-abiding and industrious. But he criticized the Norwegians, the Swedes, and the "old Texans" for the practice of sending to Europe for servants who had to work a whole year to repay the cost of a ticket ($50). "This is too reminiscent of slavery." The names of the young Scandinavians amused him. For replies by Texans, see B. G. Olsen, in *Norden*, March 11, 1884; Elise Wærenskjold, in *Norden*, May 20, 1884 (printed immediately following in the present volume); and the editors' appendix to her communication, in which they describe the violent reaction of the Texans.

Minnesota. He immediately got a very good position in Dallas. We have also had a visit from one of Mother's relatives. He was also a very cultured and fine person. His father, Emil Meldahl, lives in West Virginia, and the son, Tony, is a steamboat pilot on the Ohio River. This pays well but is very dangerous and strenuous. He liked Texas so well that it is possible he will return and buy a farm here. He also visited Otto, and his cousin Marie Wolz in Waco.

Otto and Ophelia are talking of visiting us this summer. If I go west this year it will not be until fall, because I want to get some good out of the fruit, and indications are that this will be a good fruit year.

I hope these lines will find you all well. Please greet all members of your family, your relatives, and other friends in Bosque from

Your devoted friend,

ELISE WÆRENSKJOLD

Texas and the Texans [18]

[PRAIRIEVILLE P.O.

Spring, 1884]

[TO THE EDITOR:]

Some time ago I read a letter in *Norden* from Manor, Texas, and have long expected to see something from our countrymen in Bosque by way of correction, but since nothing has appeared yet, I will take the liberty of making some remarks.

Apparently Mr. A.U. has not only taken all possible pains to ferret out every shady aspect of life in Texas but has also exaggerated matters considerably. That a man who finds everything and everybody so worthy of censure still chooses to remain in Texas strikes me as peculiar, and I will give him the good advice to go back where he came from. I have lived in Texas thirty-seven years, and it was exactly because of the mild winters that I decided to settle here. It is true that we have a few cold days during that season, and

---

[18] As was mentioned in note 17, this letter appeared in *Norden*, May 20, 1884, replying to an earlier communication by Andreas Underthun ("A.U.").

they come very suddenly; but the cold spell never lasts long and it is nothing in comparison with the severe winters up north. The thermometer (Fahrenheit) did not register lower than 4° above zero the coldest morning last winter, and it is not often that it drops that low. We had snow only twice; it stayed two days the first time and one the second. By the end of January I had already planted peas, carrots, lettuce, etc., which we have now been eating for some time. The winter was unusually dry, but now we are getting almost too much rain. Mulberries and cherries are beginning to ripen; and from now until the coming of frost we shall have several varieties of fruit, both in the orchard and growing wild.

As for me, I am well satisfied with Texas and the Texans. It is by no means so hot in Texas as many people imagine. Usually we have a pleasant breeze from the Gulf of Mexico, which moderates the weather. Only on a few days does the thermometer register 100°, and sunstroke is hardly ever heard of. To judge by Mr. A.U.'s description of the houses, he must have come in touch primarily with the poorest part of the population, or else with newcomers who have not had time to orient themselves. The native Texans in our community have good houses and are very fine neighbors — dependable and ready to help when needed. Manor is close to our capital, and if I had not read accounts by cultured Scandinavians who have lived in Austin many years, namely, Svante Palm, the consul, and Mr. Buaas — both of whom describe conditions quite otherwise — A.U. might have tempted me to believe that all the world's rogues had congregated there. But I suppose this must be accepted merely as an outburst caused by his sour mood.

I believe that theft and robbery occur much less frequently here than in most other countries. Consequently it is quite usual for us to sleep with windows and doors open during the summer. I am well aware of the fact that horse stealing is not uncommon in western Texas, but anyone would know that it is a gross exaggeration to say that whole settlements club together in gangs as horse thieves. It is unfortunately true that murderers are punished too lightly, but not more lightly here than in other states, as can be plainly seen in the papers. I will merely refer to the recent happenings in Cincinnati. It is also true that justice is corrupted by money and other influences; but this happens throughout the United States. We need only remember the Whisky Ring under Grant, the Star Route frauds, and much else.[19]

It is not Texas and Texans alone, however, that are the objects of A.U.'s censure and criticism. His countrymen in Bosque, who showed him all friendliness and hospitality, also receive their share. First, there are the names of some Norwegian children that he jokes about. It is true that some of them are odd and not happily chosen, but that is no excuse for ridiculing them publicly in a paper; and evidently it is not proper for the Norwegian women to be called "madam," but whether he finds this to be too grand or too humble a title, I am unable to tell.

When A.U. calls it slavery to work a year for one's passage across the Atlantic, he approaches the shameless. This is, of course, a voluntary agreement between two parties, and it seems to me that the risk rests entirely with the person who sends money to Norway to get a young man or woman to work for a year. It is true that this is getting help cheaper than we can hire it here, but the whole sum has to be paid in advance and it may happen — as it has — that the person who is sent for dies before his arrival or shortly thereafter, and at times I suppose it may occur that the recipient is dishonest and skips out. In both instances the money is lost. On the other hand, what do boys and girls risk who come across in this manner? Nothing, so far as I can see. If they were to work in Norway long enough to save the necessary money, it would surely take them several years, while in this way they get by with one. I would feel I was doing our poor countrymen in Norway a favor if I were in a position to help them in this way.

ELISE WÆRENSKJOLD

[19] The "Whisky Ring" (exposed 1875) and the "Star Route frauds" (exposed 1881) were notorious swindles perpetrated against the Federal government. In both cases high government officials and great sums of money were involved. In Cincinnati William Berner had killed his employer in cold blood, and was convicted of manslaughter, instead of first-degree murder. Public opinion was so intense in March, 1884, that people rioted, burned the courthouse, and destroyed records. The street fighting resulted in loss of life and the governor sent the militia to restore order. Philip D. Jordan, *Ohio Comes of Age, 1873–1900*, 185, 198 (Carl Wittke, ed., *History of the State of Ohio*, vol. 5 — Columbus, 1943).

I Enjoy Reading

PRAIRIEVILLE
July 14, 1884

DEAR THORVALD DANNEVIG:

Some time ago I received by mail six books that I presume you were so wonderfully kind as to send me and for which I heartily thank you. I have always enjoyed reading, and still do. One of your most lauded writers does not appeal to me at all, however, and he is Ibsen. I suppose the fault is mine, since he is so generally admired. I like Lie, Janson, and Kielland much better, and find Gløersen's *Laura* especially interesting.[20] I had not heard of Gløersen before I received this book from [I.T.] Relling, the book dealer; but it is remarkable how far he goes in championing the cause of women. Relling and [F.A.] Husher are kind enough to send me their papers, *Norden* and *Fædrelandet og emigranten*, free. In them are stories by Norwegian, Swedish, and Danish authors, and currently a story, *Dagny*, by Mrs. Aubert, which I like especially. She, too, is a writer about whom I have heard nothing.[21]

The last newspaper brought us the unexpected report that Johan Sverdrup had become prime minister. I wonder if things will not be more peaceful in Norway now. I mean that the Conservatives and the Liberals will probably not be so hostile and hateful toward each

[20] Kristofer Janson (1841–1917) was once widely read but is now remembered as only a minor figure. He was a tireless champion of many causes: political liberalism, Unitarianism, the New Norse language, popular education, and the folk high-school movement. He spent several years in the United States and for some time served as a Unitarian minister in Minneapolis and Hanska, Minnesota.

Alexander Kielland (1849–1906) was one of Norway's leading novelists. He is known for the elegance and delicacy of his style, but even more for his attacks on the governing bureaucracy, the capitalistic classes, old educational methods, and what he considered the hypocrisy of the state church.

Ole Kristian Gløersen (1833–1916), one of Norway's minor poets, had a considerable following in the last two decades of the nineteenth century. One of his most famous novels, *Sigurd*, is an attack on the conservative and pietistic system of rearing and educating the young. This story ran in *Norden* in 1878. Gløersen, a champion of woman's rights, attacked the double standard of morality in *Laura* (1883).

[21] Elise Sofie Aubert (1857–1909) is probably best known for various collections of letters, sketches, and short stories that described Norwegian life in the latter part of the nineteenth century. But she first became known through a series of articles in *Morgenbladet*, published during the 1870's, in which she discussed the upbringing and education of young women. Her most famous novel is undoubtedly *Dagny* (1883), in which she championed independence for her sex.

other as formerly. It has hurt me deeply to think of the recent conditions in my dear fatherland; I should be most happy if they could improve.[22]

We live tolerably well, and I thank God for unusually good health in my old age. I live with my youngest son [Niels] on our old farm, which now belongs to him. His health is not good, but he has three active children. And his wife is not well. Otto, who is a merchant in Hamilton, about one hundred and fifty miles farther [south]west, visited us recently. He too has three children; he has had eight in all. He and his wife are not in good health either.

A couple of months ago twelve Norwegians came to Four Mile Prairie. They were my husband's oldest sister (a widow Syvertsen), her son, and her son-in-law, Skjolden, with his wife and four children, besides two boys and two girls who do not belong to the family. Skjolden bought a farm about a mile from us; my sister-in-law rents a room from her sister [Elisabeth Wattner], who has lived here very close to us for some time. They are all in pretty good circumstances and are quite well satisfied and in fairly good health, for which I am very glad, because often newcomers become sick and dissatisfied.[23]

We had a delightful, but entirely unexpected, visit from one of my husband's relatives, Nils Wærenskjold, an engineer, son of Captain Frederik Wærenskjold of Christiania. He secured a position in Dallas with the land department of the Texas Pacific Railroad. And, one of my mother's relatives [Tony Meldahl] from West Virginia, cheered us with a visit this winter. Maybe it would interest you to hear a little about your acquaintances in Texas. I suppose the only ones you know here are Mother Pabst (formerly Bache) and Mother Reiersen (nee Ørbeck). Mother Pabst is really prosperous and Mother Reiersen is also well-to-do. Sigurd Ørbeck lives in Shreveport, Louisiana, and is doing well.

[ELISE WÆRENSKJOLD]

[22] Johan Sverdrup (1816–92) organized the Liberal party and led the fight for the introduction of the parliamentary system of government in Norway.

[23] Emilie Syvertsen was accompanied on the trip to Texas by her son Oscar and by John Skjolden and his wife Fanny (Emilie's daughter) and the four Skjolden children, besides the four children who were not relatives. The Wattners lived across the road from the Wærenskjold property. Emilie later built a house on land given her by Niels. Information about the house was furnished by Mrs. Fannie Webb of Amarillo, Texas (Francis Wærenskjold, daughter of Niels); Mrs. Gould to the editor, January 20, 1961.

Hard Times[24]

PRAIRIEVILLE
December 3, 1886

To the Editor:

I have recently returned from an extended visit to Hamilton and Bosque counties, and I wish to send you a few lines, since it may interest your readers to hear a little news from Texas. I have now been living in Texas for more than thirty-nine years, and I can say without exaggeration that this is the hardest year we have had since I first came here. As you have seen by the newspapers, some districts have suffered very badly from droughts, while others have suffered even more from floods. God be praised, we in the Norwegian settlements have been spared such tribulations! Yet the harvest has been smaller than usual everywhere because of an exceptionally difficult and dry summer. Moreover, the price of cotton is very low, and there has been almost no market for cattle, even though the price for them, too, is low.

Several of my friends in Bosque had died since I was there two years ago; namely, the following: my very dear friend, Aslak Nielsen from Omli Parish, father-in-law of Pastor Rystad; Mrs. Gina Hallin, who was the youngest sister of [Johan Reinert], the editor; Mrs. Berthe Foss from Toten; Mrs. Johnson from Hisøy at Arendal; and Knudsen, from the Stavanger area. All these were old and were among the earliest settlers in Texas. Furthermore, Mrs. Andrea Knudsen, a daughter of Ole Pedersen and the wife of a son of the above-mentioned Knudsen; Mrs. Siri Svendsen, a daughter of old Salve Knudsen, from the parish of Omli; and Mrs. Gina Hansen, daughter of the late Johan Brunstad from Hedmark, has also died. These last three were young wives and leave little children behind them. A very sad death occurred by accident while I was in Bosque. A young married man was fatally injured when his horse ran away; he died the following day. He was the son of Kristian Knudsen from Næs Foundry and leaves behind him his widow and a small child.

[24] This letter appeared in *Fædrelandet og emigranten*, December 21, 1886.

As the Norwegian settlement in Bosque is quite large, numbering about two thousand Scandinavians, most of whom belong to the Lutheran Church, it has been necessary to use a school building, in addition to the older church, for divine services. But now a church is being built in an appropriate location [*Norse*], and a cemetery has already been laid out close by. In addition to the church in Bosque, the Norwegians have also built churches in the town of Waco and in the settlement in Brownsboro and here at Four Mile Prairie. In our settlement the first Norwegian church was built in 1854. At that time we got a pastor [*A. E. Fridrichsen*] from Norway. He served the congregations here and in Brownsboro for three years and also visited Bosque. From this it will be seen how much truth there is in the statement in Elling Eielsen's biography that we had no divine services in Texas till Eielsen arrived here. In the same book are found several offensive and inaccurate statements about the Norwegians in Texas, which I would be loath to believe that old Elling Eielsen himself had made, since I know that we were all happy to see him among us and received him with all possible kindness.[25]

Last summer, at the expense of the Norwegians in Texas, a marble monument was erected on the grave of old Cleng Peerson in the cemetery in Bosque. It will be recalled that Peerson must be regarded as the father of Norwegian emigration to America. As early as 1821 he came to America, and after a three-year stay here he returned to Norway. His descriptions of America stimulated fifty-three persons from Stavanger to buy a sloop and sail to America in 1825. Those who believe that it was also Cleng Peerson who caused the Norwegians to move to Texas are mistaken, since both I myself and several others were already living here when old Cleng came to us, which was, so far as I recall, in 1850 or perhaps a little earlier. The man who called the attention of the Norwegians to Texas was Johan Reinert Reiersen, who had been the editor of *Christianssandsposten*. Encouraged by several people, he left for the Northern states and Texas in 1843 to investigate which state would be most advantageous for Norwegians to settle in. After his return he published his *Veiviser*. In 1845 he, with several members of his family and some others, emi-

[25] The biography referred to is Brohaugh and Eisteinsen, *Kortfattet beretning*. Pages 89–93 deal with Eielsen's visit to Texas in 1859. The book presents Texas as a rough frontier community. On A. E. Fridrichsen, see part 1, n. 11.

grated to Texas and there founded the Norwegian settlement in Brownsboro, which was then called Normandy.[26]

Besides Lutherans, there are also a few Adventists in Bosque, and several persons who do not belong to any particular congregation. There are also some Methodists among the Swedes; on the train I met some Swedish Methodist preachers, one of whom lives in Bosque. I then learned that there are six Swedish Methodist ministers in Texas and that they were to have a conference in Dallas, where there are said to be quite a few Swedes and some Norwegians. In Austin there are a great many Swedes, and there are large Swedish settlements in the vicinity of Austin, but I know very little about them.[27]

If I have tired you with this long letter, you must forgive me.

Sincerely yours,

Elise Wærenskjold

A Disastrous Year

PRAIRIEVILLE
December 31, 1886

To Mrs. Thomine Dannevig:

This has been the most disastrous year for Texas since I came to this country. Over the whole area we have suffered more or less from drought, so the crops were poor — in some counties so poor that people had to ask for help. Besides, the price of cotton was unusually low, and there was no market for livestock. Unfortunately, my husband's nephew had speculated in cattle; last year he purchased Ouline Reiersen's for $400, and tomorrow he must pay $500 on his land. If he could have sold the cattle this year, there would have been no difficulty. To help him, his sister-in-law called in a part of the money I had borrowed from her, because if he does not pay he may lose the farm. Niels owes me as much as I owe others, but how he could

---

[26] Reiersen's "Guide" is mentioned *ante*, Introduction, n. 1.
[27] The Swedes were much more numerous in Texas than the Norwegians. In 1890 there were 2,806 Swedes and 1,313 Norwegians; in 1950 there were 2,346 Swedes and 928 Norwegians. *United States Census*, 1890, 1950, *Population*; figures furnished by the University of Minnesota Libraries.

repay in such a year as this I cannot imagine. Therefore, he too had to go to a town to raise a loan. It is so disagreeable to be poor; but I must thank God so long as I have food and clothing, however simple.

My son [Niels] has moved into the house that was Otto's, and for the time being I am alone in my old home. But after New Year's a family that rents land from Niels will move into the other part of my house. I will have a living room and a kitchen for myself. Ouline [Reiersen] has sold her place for $2,000. She is to enjoy the interest — 10 per cent — on this sum as long as she lives. Niels's health is not good and Otto's even poorer. When I visited him [Otto] in September, he had just been operated on for hemorrhoids and was suffering a good deal. In the fall he became constable and, later, deputy sheriff. I do not know how large the remuneration for these offices is, but I do know that great danger is involved; it is not unusual for a deputy sheriff to be killed, for he has to arrest criminals and every disturber of the peace. Such people are not to be trifled with. At the same time I visited Otto I called on old friends in Bosque and was away nearly three months.

I have recently read *Kommandørens døttre* and Gløersen's *Daglig-dags*, both of which interested me very much, whereas I did not at all like Bjørnson's *Over ævne*. I have now subscribed to *Illustreret ugeblad*, edited by a Dane, C. Rasmussen. It is the best Norwegian-American paper I know.[28]

As you perhaps remember, I shall soon be seventy-three years old, and I am writing this without glasses, by lamplight. In the evening I read and write; during the day I sew. If I don't have anything to do for myself, I help my relatives or visit the neighbors. I have kind, pleasant neighbors, both Norwegians and Americans. I have always

[28] Jonas Lie's *Kommandørens døttre* (The Commodore's Daughters — 1886), like his more famous novel, *Familien paa Gilje* (The Family at Gilje), argues that women as well as men must have "something to live for."

Over ævne I (Beyond Human Power — 1883), Bjørnson's dramatic and controversial masterpiece, was an attack upon supernaturalistic religion, which the author claimed made too great a demand upon life and resulted in an unhealthy overstraining of human powers. The Roman numeral distinguishes this play from a later one with the same title but a different theme.

Christian Rasmussen (1852–1926) was one of the most influential publishers among Scandinavians in the United States. He emigrated from Denmark and settled in Chicago, where he lived until he moved to Minneapolis in 1887. Shortly after arriving in Chicago, he organized the C. Rasmussen Publishing Company, which began issuing *Illustreret ugeblad* (Illustrated Weekly), in 1881.

On Gløersen, author of *Dagligdags* (Everyday Life), see *ante*, n. 20.

been fortunate enough to have good friends wherever I have been, and that is a great blessing.

You must be so kind as to greet all those who may care to receive a greeting from me. If I mentioned all whom I am interested in, it would be too many. If you receive this in Tønsberg, let Lovise Seeberg read it; she sometimes delights me with an interesting letter. Lerche, too, writes now and then.

[ELISE WÆRENSKJOLD]

We Are All Well

PRAIRIEVILLE
January 21, 1887

DEAR MARIE:

When I tried today to determine from the ministerial book when your father died, I found that it only recorded his birth in Lauenburg, March 1, 1815, but did not give the date of his death. But as your mother surely remembers this, you must be so kind as to let me know as soon as possible, so that Wattner can finish the matter [cemetery lot?]. Still no little one at Niels's. We are all well and hope to hear the same from you. Johnsen has built a house beside his father-in-law Simon. Ouline R. lives with Gunhild Knudsen. Happy New Year to you all.

[ELISE WÆRENSKJOLD]

[Marginal note:] Write soon! Send the money in the form of a money order to Wills Point.

I Am Hard Up

PRAIRIEVILLE
February 13, 1887

DEAR MARIE:

Many thanks for the letter! And Knud Hansen has passed away. The old Four Mile people are disappearing rapidly — five since the young girls and I visited you. I believe that Hansen was satisfied to leave, but there is something eerie about such a sudden death.

How goes it with Ottesen and Adventism? Greet Christopher warmly for me and give him and his wife my heartiest congratulations. Little did I suspect when I visited him that he was the other suitor, but before I left Bosque it was rumored to me in all secrecy that Cora would probably be married. How did the children like getting a stepmother? How is Mrs. Haagestøl getting along without Oli?

A twelve-pound boy [*Niels Anthony*] was born to Niels January twenty-sixth. All is well, and the wife of one of the renters is there to take care of the house. She is a kind woman and has no children.

Anton and Mina [Aanonsen] are in their house; I have not been there yet. Johnsen, who is married to Simon's daughter, built close to Simon's and has also moved in. I have not seen the house. The child died before they moved from Canton.

I am sure that $5 will pay for everything. If Andreas [Staack] could at the same time send me the $1.50 for the album, he would do me a great service, because I am extremely hard up.

Yesterday and last night we had a very good rain, and now the sun is shining — everything will grow well. It has been a good winter for the animals and also for plowing.

Greet your dear mother very warmly for me, and you and your family and other friends are most sincerely greeted from your ever devoted

ELISE WÆRENSKJOLD

Babies Are Born

PRAIRIEVILLE
May 16, 1887

DEAR MARIE:

I should have written to you a long time ago, but I wanted to wait until I could get your father's grave fixed. This took a longer time than I had expected because one must go so far for bricks that it would not pay to hire a man merely to bring the few needed for the grave. The work was done, however, before the minister [*Pastor Torrison*] came; I hope it will last through many years, as we used walnut, which is said to be more lasting than cedar. In the second place, I wanted to wait until the minister had been here so that I would have something to write about. Otherwise nothing happens here except that babies are born now and then. Of these there are no less than four to report this time; and the remarkable thing is that each of these four babies has one Norwegian and one American parent. The children belong to Oscar Andersen, Julie Small, Johnnie Pedersen, and my Niels. Oscar does not want to have his child baptized, and the Pedersens are going to wait until the minister comes again. Julie named the child for her mother, but neither she [*Tulla*] nor Aanon wanted to see their little granddaughter baptized. Niels's boy was named Niels Anthony Walter for his papa, for Tony Meldahl, and for a little deceased brother of Babe's.

We had a beautiful service a week ago yesterday. First Carl Wattner, Emilie Pedersen, Tina Jordahl, and Nielsine Aanonsen were confirmed, and in the afternoon we had Communion. Most of us brought food along and ate together; we had a good and enjoyable dinner; but some were what I would call odd, and they went home to eat. The Communion sermon was one of the best I have heard in a long time. We like our minister better every time he comes here.

Mrs. [Gunhild] Knudsen has been sick with bronchitis but has begun to sit up. Ouline Reiersen makes her home with her and they have a pleasant life together. Mina and Anton were there yesterday; they are getting along well.

We have had sufficient rain up to now and everything seems much alive. Niels has six renters and a hired man — all white folks and, I believe, good workers. A kind, pleasant woman, Mrs. Bennett, lives in the same house with me, and we are very congenial. Babe and the children are quite friendly, now that we do not stay together, so things are more pleasant for me than they have been for a long time. There are so many good things in the garden. I have eaten asparagus almost every day from the third of March until yesterday, when I gave it up. We also have peas, beans, turnips, carrots, squash, spinach, and other things — I practically live off the garden. In a couple of weeks my chickens will be large enough to eat, and I will undoubtedly get enough of them this year. Last year I had none, but now I have about fifty. I expect to get two months of schoolteaching this year because several people who do not have children themselves signed up for contributions anyway, the minister himself pledging $1.50.

Some time ago I heard that gold had been discovered on Gran's land. Is this true? How I wish that I could be in Bosque tomorrow and take part in the Seventeenth of May celebrations, but that is only a vain hope, partly because I cannot be away from home at this time of year and also because I have no money. If I had not collected $.15 yesterday I would not have had enough even to buy stamps for this letter. I do wish that Andreas [Staack] would send the $1.50 he owes me. He can, of course, get a little money order or postal note in Clifton.

Next time you cheer me with a letter, you must give me all the news from Bosque. I have not for the longest time had a letter from anyone there, and [Pastor] Torrison knows so little about Bosque. I believe he is better acquainted here at Four Mile, since he goes about and visits all of us. He had dinner twice with me. I must report that by chance I learned that Fritz Hansen is still alive, but that is about all I know. A widow, a Mrs. Wærenskjold, who would like to come to Texas (and in that connection wrote to me), talked with him in Copenhagen. He told her that he knew me and corresponded with me, but the correspondence with Mr. Hansen is, to be sure, a one-way arrangement, as it is five years or more since I last had a letter from him.

I would like very much to know how all of you are getting along. How is Christopher? Do Ole and his grown-up daughters get along well together? Was Inger Grimeland's baby a boy or a girl? Has a little one arrived at Andreas'? Do you hear anything about the Wilsens? Greet all my friends in Bosque and especially your dear mother. Did your uncle [Knud Hansen] become a freethinker before he died — as a freethinker delivered the funeral sermon — and what was the sermon like? But it is high time that I end my letter, with a heartfelt greeting to you and your family from

Your devoted
ELISE WÆRENSKJOLD

Today I Started the School

PRAIRIEVILLE
June 27, 1887

DEAR MARIE:

Many thanks for your friendly letter, which I received day before yesterday. I was glad to hear that you are all well and especially that a little Mr. Staack has arrived. You must give his parents and his grandmother my congratulations on having a son and a grandson. I hope he will become the forefather of many Staacks.[29]

We had already heard the news about the boy at Mrs. By's, but what is her connection with Jacob Hansen? I have long expected to hear that some of the many engaged couples in Bosque would celebrate weddings, but so far have heard nothing. Probably I can get to some of them if I can scratch together enough for the fare to Bosque and Hamilton. Today I started the school, but what I earn goes to Anton Aa [nonsen]. Ask Andreas [Staack] to send the money by Helene Pedersen, who will stay in Bosque a month. Since she will be able to tell all the news from here, I will merely say that life goes on as usual, which means tolerably well. I have another letter to write, so I close with a cordial greeting to you and the others from

Your devoted
ELISE WÆRENSKJOLD

An Old Cat, a Few Chickens, Some Turkeys [30]

PRAIRIEVILLE
December 20, 1887

TO MADAM BASBERG:

Things are well with me now — yes, much better than I could expect and better than I deserve, and I cannot thank God enough,

---

[29] "Little Mr. Staack" was Marion, son of Andreas, Marie Staack Jensen's brother. The grandmother was Madam Staack; Mrs. Price to the editor, January 24, 1961.

[30] This letter appeared in *Tønsbergs blad*, May 23, 1925, with the group of Dannevig letters. Madam Basberg has not been identified.

who arranges everything so well for me. From New Year's on I shall have $80 a year and a free house, garden, wood, and pork, and on that I can live quite well in my old age. It was just this fall that I made this arrangement with my children. Since I have turned everything over to them, I now have nothing but an old cat, a few chickens, and some turkeys. I have a living room and a kitchen for myself, and the people who live in the other part of the house are kind and agreeable. In the fall I usually visit Otto and my friends in Bosque, as I did this year, too.

At Bosque I attended an unusual wedding, unusual in that one son and two daughters of a wealthy widow were married at the same time. There were about five hundred guests. We met at the church and from there went to the house of the brides and had dinner. Many stayed there for the evening meal too, because there was to be dancing at night. I also went to another large wedding where we had a very nice time. There are so many in Bosque who once lived here at Four Mile Prairie. Several of the women have worked for me, and when I come to visit them it is as if I came to relatives — we have such a very cozy time together. The Norwegians have two churches in Bosque, one in Waco, one here, and one in Brownsboro; and we have two pastors [Rystad and Torrison].

Yesterday was a wonderfully mild day, and I am so happy that I washed clothes, because during the night a blustery north wind came up and today water froze in my kitchen.

At times I think how much fun it would be to spend a few months in Norway and stay with you in Christiania and have some of the good food you know so well how to prepare. I miss the delicious fish of Norway so much. I have not eaten fish cakes since we lay in Drøbak, waiting for a favorable wind.

[ELISE WÆRENSKJOLD]

I Miss Books

TO MRS. THOMINE DANNEVIG:

My heartfelt thanks for your welcome letter and the many reports concerning our mutual acquaintances. You are extremely fortunate, indeed, to be able to visit your children. Both of us are getting too old to travel much; but it is so good to be with one's own children. I cannot thank God enough, who gives us sufficient strength in our old age to do this. Yes, God has mercifully directed everything for my good; frequently what looked very threatening turned into a blessing for me.

I had borrowed $150 to pay a debt but had more than that due me. Then my loan was unexpectedly called in while I could not collect what was owed me. I was forced to try to get the money from a bank with good security; but this was more difficult than I had thought. The guarantor demanded not only a mortgage on my sheep and cattle, but I had to promise him also to attempt to borrow the money in Norway. I then wrote to Foyn, briefly explaining my situation, and, just think, he was so extremely kind as to send me $400! There is perhaps not one man in a thousand — no, hardly one in a million — who would do as much for a divorced wife as Foyn has done for me. I was so happy that I slept very little that night.

Now I have made arrangements with my children to live in my old house without worry for the future. Things will be simple and frugal, as are my clothes, but you know that I have never been fond of luxury. Most I miss no longer being able to afford books. Occasionally I am presented with one or two as gifts. Thus, last Christmas I received *Amtmandens døttre* by Camilla Collett, from a Danish cousin, and Oscar Reiersen, the oldest son of the editor, gave me Bjørnson's *Det flager i byen og paa havnen*. Kristofer Janson has sent me quite a few of his books too.[31]

[ELISE WÆRENSKJOLD]

[31] Jacobine Camilla Collett (1813–95) was a sister of the famous Norwegian poet Henrik Wergeland. She became well known as Norway's first prominent champion of

I Could Write Much about Texas [32]

PRAIRIEVILLE, TEXAS
September 3, 1888

[TO THE EDITOR:]

I have read with much interest several issues of *Posten*, which, as you know, comes to Prairieville; they are like a greeting from the old homeland. Since I notice that you have printed a couple of letters from Texas, I thought your readers might like to have a few lines from a woman who has lived here for forty-one years.

Texas is the largest state in the Union; it is larger than France and Germany, and, next to Florida, it is the southernmost of the states. As to climate, it is quite varied, which you will readily understand because the area is so vast. The pleasant breeze from the Gulf of Mexico tempers the summer heat so that it is seldom oppressive; sunstroke occurs very seldom. The winter is short and usually mild and pleasant, but we may also have really severe days — or, more often, nights — with north winds and penetrating cold.

Toward the end of January and the beginning of February we can start planting gardens, and by early March we have asparagus to eat. But it goes without saying that the products, like the climate, of so vast an area are diversified. In the southern part of the state cotton, sugar, rice, sweet potatoes, and oranges are raised, but in the part where we Norwegians have settled, rice and oranges cannot be produced. A little sugar cane is raised for syrup, which, however, is prepared primarily from sorghum, a plant that grows and is cultivated like Indian corn. A great amount of the latter is raised both for bread and for fodder. Wheat, rye, barley, oats, and all sorts of vege-

woman's rights and was the anonymous author of *Amtmandens døttre* (The Governor's Daughters), the earliest novel of social purpose in Norway (1854–55). In it she attacked the conventional view of marriage that ignored woman's feelings and her rights as a personality.

Bjørnson's *Det flager i byen og paa havnen* (Flags Are Flying in Town and Harbor — 1884) appeared in English in 1890 as *The Heritage of the Kurts*. It championed new departures in such fields as education and government, but was especially vehement in condemning the double standard of morality. On Janson, see *ante*, n. 20.

[32] This letter appeared October 12, 1888, in *Posten*, a newspaper published variously from Christiania, Kongsvinger, and Skien, 1888–93, which described itself as an organ for "progress, freedom and peace." A photostatic copy was furnished by Professor Kenneth O. Bjork.

tables do especially well; the same can be said about peaches, apples, pears, plums, and other fruits. There are many kinds of grapes, several of them growing wild. We also have wild plums and a very sweet fruit known as persimmons, which resemble dates. Pecans are the most important nuts, and great quantities of them are sold in other states.

There are numerous cattle, horses, mules, sheep, hogs, and goats in the state, and in later years animals of superior breeds have been brought in. But the income from animal husbandry is not nearly so great now as it was a few years ago, for the prices of both cattle and wool have declined considerably — besides, it costs more and more to feed stock through the winter. When we first came here, no one had to worry about feeding the animals because the grass was extremely good and only cultivated land was fenced; but now weeds have largely replaced the grass, and fences surround all types of land — fields, meadows, pastures. Sheep, goats, and hogs are not permitted to stray onto another man's fenced area. This may still happen, however, because the animals can slip through the wire fences that people use here. Conditions are not nearly so good for poor people now as when we came; at that time they could acquire animals without owning land. I suppose poor people are found in all parts of the world, but we have no poverty here in the Norwegian sense of the word, nor any poor rate, nor begging.

The wages for unmarried people are good. They get $15 a month plus board for common farm work, while in the towns a girl may receive from $15 to $25 a month as an ordinary housemaid.

When we came here people used to travel by oxcart, but now rail-roads cross the country in all directions. Instead of the poor shelters, which one of the Texas letters describes with much exaggeration, the houses now are generally good. It is true that our church is simple, but it is a large white building with three big windows on either side extending up toward the eaves. One cannot in justice expect more, considering that our Norwegian congregation on Four Mile Prairie (in Kaufman and Van Zandt counties) numbers only nineteen families. Here the first Norwegian church in Texas was built — in 1854 — but it was torn down long ago. There is another little Norwegian settlement in the neighboring county, Henderson, which also has its own church. The largest Norwegian settlement [in Texas] is located in Bosque County, about a hundred and twenty English (seventeen Norwegian) miles [south] west of us. Many of the Norwegian settlers are well off, and they have substantial, beautiful churches. Pastor Rystad lives in Bosque County. We have another Norwegian minister [*Torrison*] who lives in Waco, a large railway center a day's journey with horses from the settlement in Bosque. About two thousand Scandinavians, mostly Norwegians, live in the latter place. In Austin, the capital of Texas, there are more Swedes than Norwegians. In the Williamson County area there are large flourishing Swedish settlements. There is also a little Danish settlement — in Limestone County, I believe. The Norwegian pastors, Rystad and Torrison, visit us and also Norwegians in Henderson County two or three times a year.[33]

People back home believe that there are many thieves and scoundrels in America, but these usually come from other countries. During the summer we sleep with open windows and doors, and we can leave our houses without locking up, so you will realize that we do not have as great fear of thieves as they have in the old country.

Tyler is a large town about fifty miles from us, where there was an exposition recently that we visited. Several Norwegian families are located there. They live in prosperous circumstances and are highly respected. I can mention a certain man who is the son of one of the poorest families that ever came over from Norway to America: he [*S. Christian Halvorsen*] married the governor's daughter, and all his sisters also married well.

Many other things I could write about Texas, but now I must close with the best wishes for my beloved fatherland and its future.

ELISE WÆRENSKJOLD

[33] On Rystad, see *ante*, n. 8. Isaac Bertinius Torrison (1859–1929) served his first pastorate in Waco, Texas, 1885–89. Thereafter he was pastor in Chicago, St. Louis, and Decorah, Iowa. He taught at Luther College in Decorah, 1902–12.

Two Papers from Norway

PRAIRIEVILLE P.O.
October 19, 1888

To Mrs. THOMINE DANNEVIG:

Thanks for the information regarding the Aalls. Old Jacob Aall's wife was my father's cousin, and since his parents died while he was a child, the two [cousins] were brought up together and thought of each other as brother and sister.

Both Ouline Reiersen and Mother Pabst are well and greet you cordially. I dropped in on the latter for a few hours on my return from a visit to Otto's.

I am so very fond of vegetables that I always have a well-kept garden. I think it is healthful to eat and to work among growing things. We have lots of asparagus and can eat it every day from the first of March until May. Even earlier than that we have turnips, peas, and carrots. Yes, turnips and carrots can be had all winter long. But there is one thing I miss here — and that is the delicious fish you have in Norway.

I read Arctander's lecture given in the hall of the Labor Union and am really annoyed by it. I hope that some Norwegian American will come up with a reply. His statements are grossly exaggerated. We read two papers from Norway. I subscribe to *Nylænde* and one of my relatives takes *Posten*; both are edited by women.[34]

The elder of our two pastors [*Rystad*] is with us now. One resides in Bosque, where there are two Norwegian churches, and the other [*Torrison*] lives in Waco. One or the other comes to us several times a year. Each time he delivers sermons on three Sundays and two weekdays, besides officiating at baptisms, weddings, and the like.

---

[34] John W. Arctander (1849–1920), prominent journalist and lawyer, went to Chicago from Norway in 1870. He soon moved to Minneapolis, where he was connected with Norwegian-American publications and developed a successful law practice. The lecture mentioned by Mrs. Wærenskjold took place in Christiania. It was critical of the United States, and aroused considerable ire among Norwegian Americans.

Nylænde (New Frontiers) was published in Christiania by Norsk Kvindesagsforening (Norwegian Society for Woman's Rights), 1887–1927. Jørgine (Gina) Krog edited it until 1916. Largely because of her intellectual leadership, Norway became in 1913 the first country to establish political equality between the sexes; information furnished by Professor Kenneth O. Bjork. On *Posten*, see n. 32.

After a long period of the loveliest autumn weather one can imagine — so favorable for picking cotton — it now looks as if there will be a change. All in all this has been a good year, but last winter was the worst one I have ever experienced.

I had almost forgotten to tell you that bad luck overtook Sigurd Ørbeck this fall. The house in which he had lived for several years burned, and he lost everything but the clothes he had on. At the same time he lost his job, because the firm he worked for [*Reiersen and Grøgaard*] moved away from Shreveport. The Lord only knows what he will do now.

Today Niels is taking thirty cattle to Wills Point, where he will get $300 for them. This is very little compared to what they were worth a few years ago, but it is better than two years ago, when there was absolutely no market for cattle. He has over one hundred head, including the calves. Neither Ouline nor I now have any kind of animals, not even a cat. As we have no horse, we have to use the "apostles' steeds" when we want to visit neighbors. I am glad as long as I can walk, without too much effort, to Prairieville or to my other neighbors in the morning and home again in the evening. Prairieville is three miles away. I know little of the Grøgaards, but believe they are getting along quite well. Have you heard anything about the Hedemarks and the Rosenvolds, who many years ago left for Ole Bull's colony? I did have a letter from them later — from New York.[35]

[ELISE WÆRENSKJOLD]

A Christmas Present

PRAIRIEVILLE
January 23, 1889

To MRS. THOMINE DANNEVIG:

A couple of days ago I had the pleasure of receiving a letter from Augusta Lerche. As I was answering it today the desire struck me to

[35] Elise's house was in Four Mile Prairie, an area served by the Prairieville post office, which was across the line in Kaufman County. Hence the heading "Prairieville." Ole Bull's colony was the famous but ill-fated settlement, Oleana, founded by the noted Norwegian violinist in Potter County, Pennsylvania, 1852–53. See Blegen, *Norwegian Migration, 1825–1860*, chapter 13.

send you a few lines at the same time. I must tell you that our good friend Sigurd Ørbeck died, to the great sorrow of his sister [*Ouline Reiersen*]. A letter she sent him last month was returned, marked "Deceased." Presumably he died suddenly, otherwise he would have found someone to write for him. She went over there [to Shreveport] immediately. It is a hard blow for her, especially since she hoped that he might move here and share a little home with her.

Niel's wife gave me a new little granddaughter [*Mabel Claire*] on the fifteenth of this month. They have seven children now, six of their own and an orphan boy, thirteen years old, a great-grandson of Mother's youngest brother.

I received several Christmas presents and gave myself one, namely *Norske digtere*, by N. Rolfsen. I earned the money by selling subscriptions to a good American magazine. I cannot say that I am satisfied with the book, because it is far from complete. Authors that I think much of, such as Gløersen and Elise Aubert, are not mentioned, while others that I feel are less important are included. There are two books I hope I will find the means to buy : *Norsk forfatter-lexicon 1814–1880*, edited by J. B. Halvorsen, and *Fra nordens natur og folkeliv*, edited by H. G. Heggtveit. I don't think that either one is obtainable in America.[36]

At New Year's I got new tenants; I am so glad that it turned out so well, as I gained rather than lost by the exchange. I wonder if S. Foyn is going whaling again; he will be eighty in June. Can one buy a picture of him ?

Since I have come to the end of the page, I must finish with an affectionate greeting to you and yours and greetings to all my old friends.

[ELISE WÆRENSKJOLD]

[36] Johan Nordahl Bruun Rolfsen (1848–1928), Norwegian educator, writer, and editor, was best known for his textbooks for public schools. His *Norske digtere* (Norwegian Poets), an anthology of eighteenth- and nineteenth-century writers, first appeared in Christiania, 1886.

Jens Braage Halvorsen (1845–1900) librarian and literary historian, is best known for *Norsk forfatter-lexikon 1814–1880* (Lexicon of Norwegian Authors, 1814–1880), published in Christiania, a six-volume encyclopedia of brief biographies and bibliographies of Norwegian literary figures.

Hallvard G. Heggtveit (1850–1924) was a schoolman, editor, and church historian. His *Fra nordens natur og folkeliv* (Nature and Folk Life in the North — 1880) consists of Scandinavian poetry and prose selections.

In My Garden

PRAIRIEVILLE
May 10, 1889

DEAR MARIE:

Just now I had the pleasure of receiving your welcome letter and was surprised to learn that you did not get the one I wrote to you last fall.

Unfortunately I cannot remember anything about your father's family except that I know he had relatives in Germany and a brother in Denmark. I am sorry that your mother's health is not good. Here all are well, and I believe all the Norwegians were in church when the minister was here. Three children were baptized: N. Andersen's Johan Otto, Mina's Gina Christine, and Niels's Mabel Claire. Five were enrolled for confirmation: Almer Knudsen, Ole Olsen, Julius Olsen, Fredrik Wattner, and Nora Pedersen. This is all the news I have to tell you, because I am certain you already know that Berthea Eastvold, her two children, and Anne Andersen have been staying for some time at "Smed" [*Blacksmith*] Olsen's. Berthea would like to remain in Texas, but she cannot get her husband to come, so I suppose they will soon have to go back.

As for me, I am getting along quite well. I work every day in my garden and now have asparagus, peas, carrots, turnips, beets, and potatoes to eat, while the tomatoes, squash, and melons are in bloom, and my first planting of sweet corn already has tassels. So you see I have a good garden, and we have had mulberries every day for a couple of weeks. I planted raspberry and blackberry bushes and will get a few berries. I have forty-nine chickens and a hen that will set tomorrow; this will be all I need.

Niels now has four girls and two boys. The youngest boy, two years old, looks like my father. I wish Mrs. Staack could see him. Niels has bought your parents' old place from Johan Reiersen for $11.[37] Bells, who had bought it, could not pay, but now rents it from Niels. I

[37] Here Mrs. Wærenskjold apparently refers to John Reiersen, son of Johan Reinert. The latter had died in 1864.

recently had a letter from Otto, and he says that they are all well. I do not know yet if I will get out there next fall; but if I do, I will go through Bosque, rain or shine.

You must greet Ragnhild [Wilsen] and tell her that I am really angry at her and Berte because they never write to me. I think it is really mean of them. I have heard about the big wedding Cora had. You must greet her warmly for me. Tell her that I wish her all the best in her married state. Ouline Reiersen got a letter from Lina Halling that told about the wedding. I suppose you have heard that our good friend Sigurd Ørbeck is dead. Ouline visits me often when she is at home, but she travels a lot. At present she is in Palestine [Texas]. She went to Shreveport when she heard that her brother had died, and she has also been in Tyler and Kaufman.

I have reread your letter, and it seems to me that there might have been some swindle connected with your aunt's wish that the deaf-mute Christian Staack should inherit everything. If it had really been her wish that he should have it all, she could, of course, have willed it to him. Is that man Wiebeck also supposed to be a relative? I would not advise you to give up your inheritance on the strength of the word of an unknown person that this was the wish of the deceased.[38]

Finally, my sincere greetings to you and your family and my other friends from

Your devoted
ELISE WÆRENSKJOLD

[38] On the Staack family inheritance, see part 2, n. 12.

PART FOUR

Growing Old in Texas

1890–1895

I Must Rest Frequently

PRAIRIEVILLE P.O.
April 23, 1890

DEAR MARIE:

[John] Skjolden, who is married to my husband's niece, is now in Tyler, where he intends to stay. He receives $2.25 per day at B. Olsen's and pays $3 per week for board, so he is very well satisfied and wants the family to move down there. He has, in a way, sold the farm here; that is to say, if the buyer can provide the money. He has joined the field to the pasture and leased it to Knud Mjaaland for $16 per month. I will miss him very much, because Skjolden is such an interesting man to talk with. Wattner went to Dallas, where he had a job, but was so unfortunate as to injure three fingers in a machine, so he came home with the minister. The minister [Rystad] remained only three days. Otto was here for a short visit last fall and became very sick after his return home. Then he got an electric belt and has improved so much that he says he has become young again. Ouline Reiersen has moved to Prairieville and is living in Johan Reiersen's house; we see little of each other now, as the roads are almost always so muddy that we cannot walk. I have been in Prairieville only twice this year. Tulla Knudsen has been quite sick, but she is now up and around again.

This is the third day of rain, so I am unable to work in my garden. This is too bad, because the grass and weeds threaten to overpower me. I cannot work fast and must rest frequently. God willing, I hope to make my usual trip to Bosque and Hamilton.

147

Niels has been offered $8 per acre for all his land, which would total about $10,000, but he has determined to remain at Four Mile. If he had sold I would have moved to Otto's, but, of course, I prefer to remain in my old home.

Greet your dear old mother [*Madam Staack*] very warmly for me and also your relatives and friends, but special greetings to you, your husband [*Stephen Jensen*], and children from your old friend,

ELISE WÆRENSKJOLD

Prospects for a Study Club

PRAIRIEVILLE
May 16, 1890

TO THORVALD DANNEVIG:

A thousand thanks for the books! It was a real pleasure to read *Kong Midas*, which I have read about so often in the papers. I liked Bjørnson's *Paa Guds veie* very much, far better than *Det flager i byen og paa havnen*.[1] I have read a little here and there in *Fra nordens natur og folkeliv* and find it especially interesting, but regret that it contains so much Swedish; and, worse yet, there is so much New Norse [*landsmaal*].[2] In spite of my being Norwegian, body and soul, this is too Norse for me, and I can really understand the Swedish better. The Norwegian dialects differ so much from district to district that I cannot see how it will be possible to make a language from them that can be understood by all the people. During the period when emigrants were coming to Four Mile Prairie from Norway, we had many a good laugh over the misunderstandings that arose be-

[1] *Kong Midas* (King Midas), a play, was published by the Norwegian dramatist, Gunnar Heiberg, in 1890. It was presumed to be a satirical analysis of Bjørnstjerne Bjørnson's reform ideals. The novel *Paa Guds veie* (In the Paths of God) was published in 1880. It was mainly an attack on orthodox Christianity and a defense of religious tolerance. On *Det flager i byen og paa havnen* and *Fra nordens natur og folkeliv*, see *ante,* part 3, n. 31, 36.
[2] Mrs. Wærenskjold's complaint that too much space in the book was given to Swedish is hardly justified; 382 pages were devoted to Norway and only 84 to Sweden. *Landsmaal* was a linguistic creation by the self-taught peasant, Ivar Aasen (1813–96), who sought to give his country a truly Norwegian idiom by synthesizing the various dialects. In 1885 the two types of Norwegian gained equal status by law.

tween the easterners and westerners as they conversed. They all came to us and stayed for a shorter or longer time.

Prospects for our study club are poor, as the most intelligent Norwegian at Four Mile [*John Skjolden*] moved to Tyler, about fifty miles away, and my brother-in-law [*Adolph S. Wattner*] has taken employment in Dallas; another man died of the grippe. Furthermore, we had a bad season last year, and it looks as if things will be still worse, for we have had too much rain ever since the New Year. On May 3 and 4 it fell in torrents, with hail and a frightful wind that played havoc with our fields and orchards. We must, however, thank God that it was not worse, for many suffered great damage to house and furniture, and many people lost their lives. At Wills Point, only fifteen miles away, two people were killed; the big Methodist church, the schoolhouse, and the depot were completely ruined, and the other churches, as well as many houses, were damaged more or less. And yet many other places fared even worse. I am extremely anxious to hear from Hamilton and Bosque.

[ELISE WÆRENSKJOLD]

It's Really Dismal at Four Mile

PRAIRIEVILLE
July 7, 1890

To MRS. THOMINE DANNEVIG:

Many thanks for your two welcome letters, and will you convey my sincere thanks to your brother for his thoughtfulness in informing me of his wife's death? It saddens me indeed, for I realize so well what a great loss it must be for him; but perhaps it will not be too long before he can join her. What a wonderful hope it is that we may gather with our loved ones in a better world where there is neither sickness nor sorrow nor parting! How dark and hopeless it would be to contemplate the grave without this blessed consolation!

God be praised, my son Otto is now enjoying good health. He was very miserable all last year, but he got an electric belt which has worked wonders for him. He says he feels rejuvenated and is now able to work as well as anyone, and, of course, with his better health, his earning power has increased.

I plan to visit him as usual this fall, and I am looking forward to being away from Four Mile for a time. All my American friends, with the exception of one family, have left, and the relatives in whom I was most interested, John Skjolden and his wife and five children, have moved to Tyler, where they are much better off than here. It's really dismal now at Four Mile. Numerous houses are standing empty, much farm land lies uncultivated, fences are down, and orchards partially destroyed. The land in this area has been bought up for speculation by large loan companies, but I think it will prove to be a poor investment.

In Fort Worth they built what was called a "Spring Palace" last year. It was very large and exceptionally beautiful, and the whole building, inside and out, was artistically decorated with things that grow in Texas. This made the building so highly inflammable that no one was allowed to smoke in it. Nevertheless someone carelessly dropped a match on the floor, and when a little boy kicked it, a fire started and in no time the whole building was in flames. About seven thousand people were in the building when the fire broke out, but strangely enough no one was burned to death except a man who sacrificed his life working till the last to save women and children by lowering them with a rope. When the last one was safe, he tried to let himself down, but the rope was so badly burned that it broke. His clothing caught fire, and he died shortly afterward.[3]

We had an unusual season this year: when we should have had winter we had spring, and when we should have had spring, winter arrived. The peach trees, whose fruit had already formed, froze, so we will have no peaches this year, which will be a great loss. At present it is very hot and dry with the thermometer up to 100°.

Our pastor [Rystad], his wife, and three children have just visited us. Five young people were confirmed.

Your letters telling of friends and events at home are very inter-

---

[3] The "Texas Spring Palace" was erected at the instigation of General R. A. Cameron, colonization and immigration agent of the Forth Worth and Denver Railroad. It had the form of a St. Andrew's cross, with sections allotted to the various Texas counties for displaying their produce. B. B. Paddock, ed., *Fort Worth and the Texas Northwest*, 2:870–872 (Chicago and New York, 1922); citation furnished by Derwood Johnson.

esting to me. How much fun it would be to see the old places again! I wonder if the old parsonage at Moland is still standing.

Please greet all who remember me.

[ELISE WÆRENSKJOLD]

Teaching Sunday School

PRAIRIEVILLE
December 1, 1890

MY DEAR MARIE:

Many thanks both to you and your good mother for all the hospitality you showed me. I returned home yesterday after an altogether pleasant trip of eight days; I found everybody in good health and happy to see old Grandmother back again. All the local Norwegians are well, and Mrs. Knudsen has been fortunate enough to rent her place for next year.

How did it go with the books from Vickery? I hope they arrived safely. They undoubtedly are very good books, but I am not going to have anything more to do with him. I got absolutely nothing for my work, not even reimbursement for the money orders I had bought and several little things I had ordered and paid for.

Please tell me how Jens and the others like it out west and how things are going with the inheritance [*Sophie Staack's estate*]. Yesterday I began to teach Sunday school for Ole Olsen's children, Gina Pedersen, and Carl Olsen. They really need it, because they have fallen farther behind than I had expected. Anne [Olsen] sent me both butter and cheese with the children.

An American woman who has four very small children lost her mind and has been sent to an asylum in Terrell. Her husband has become sick from sorrow and overexertion. A brother of John Carlisle's wife had the great misfortune of losing his house in a fire. Everything in it, including his youngest child, was consumed by the flames.

Mrs. Clemet Gilbert, who lives with me, gave me a dishful of persimmons today. I thought they were all gone by now. There were so many beautiful roses and other flowers in full bloom in Kaufman.

I will now close with cordial greetings to all of you and especially your dear mother, as well as all my good friends. How did it go with Mrs. Cooper? Did Talma get the school?

Your always devoted
ELISE WÆRENSKJOLD

I Sent the Needles

HAMILTON
August 31, 1891

DEAR MARIE:

Svendsen was so very kind as to take me clear to Hansen's the same evening, and Hansen brought me here the next day. I found everyone well. Your letter was here also. Claud Pedersen, his two children, and his unmarried sister came here a week before me but left today, taking Lilli [Wærenskjold] along with them. Kaja Olsen gave birth to a stillborn baby.

I sent the needles with Hansen and asked him to leave them in Clifton. Be so kind as to pay the $.30 to Gunild Andersen and ask her to give his mother $.25.

Otto and family send a friendly greeting to all of you, but you especially are greeted by

Yours sincerely,
ELISE WÆRENSKJOLD

My Thoughts Are in Lillesand

PRAIRIEVILLE
July 29, 1892

To MRS. THOMINE DANNEVIG:

You can't imagine how often my thoughts are in Lillesand, and in the parsonage at Moland. It was there, of course, that I spent my happiest days. I wonder how things look at Møglestue now? I don't suppose the beautiful garden is kept up. Is the vocational school still in existence?

My life goes on in the same old way. I thank God that he gives me strength to carry on my household tasks and to work in my garden, and that I can manage to travel alone when I go to visit my dear Otto.

On May 5 a little baby girl [*Lelia Grace*] was born very suddenly to Niels — in fact, she came so suddenly that she was there before either the neighbor woman or the doctor could arrive. But all went well, and she is a very good little girl. Pastor Rystad christened her at the home of her parents, and an odd thing happened: five old women were sponsors, because the men and young women invited to be sponsors did not have time to come. Pastor Rystad arrived May 14, but it rained so hard both May 15 and 17, when we were to have had church services, that they could not be held. The minister stays here only eight days at a time — entirely too short a visit for [giving religious instruction to] the young people who are preparing for confirmation.

I suppose you have read in the newspapers of all the catastrophes that have happened in America this year: storms, cyclones, and floods. In our neighborhood, too, there have been more storms and rain than usual; but, thank God, beyond the destruction of a good many fruit trees, no damage has been done. From all appearances we will have a very bountiful harvest.

[ELISE WÆRENSKJOLD]

Many Cannot Read Norwegian [4]

PRAIRIEVILLE

KAUFMAN COUNTY, TEXAS

May 10, 1894

To PROFESSOR RASMUS B. ANDERSON.

MOST HONORABLE PROFESSOR:

I have read with great interest what you have written in *Amerika* as an introduction to accounts of immigration. I do so sincerely wish that it were in English, since many of our people here cannot read Norwegian and, unfortunately, not a few, in their ignorance, are almost ashamed of being Norwegian. I admire your warm interest in our native land and your continuing efforts to make Norway better known and to gain for her the recognition she deserves among the Americans, who are so prone to look down upon foreigners.

Sometimes I busy myself with selling books, and I have had several ask me if a history of Norway in English is obtainable. If there is such a volume, will you kindly advise me as to where it can be secured, and the price? A history of Norway up to the present, but not so lengthy as to be too expensive, would, in my opinion, be especially suitable to awaken the interest of our countrymen in the old land of their forefathers. Would you not be interested in producing such a book if one is not already available?

I was an agent for *De hjem vi forlod og de hjem vi fandt* and did not know that it could not be obtained in both languages. Several of the subscribers, as well as I myself, wanted it in English, and were very disappointed to get it in Norwegian. I have two sons, both married to Americans, who, as well as my grandchildren, do not understand Norwegian. In another respect, too, we were disappointed

---

[4] The four letters in this volume addressed to Rasmus B. Anderson are from the Anderson Papers, State Historical Society of Wisconsin at Madison. Those of July 3 and December 26, 1894, were called to the editor's attention by Professor Carlton C. Qualey of Carleton College, Northfield, Minnesota. Rasmus Bjørn Anderson (1846–1936), the well-known and controversial Norwegian-American author, took an intense interest in Norwegian culture and tried to make it better known in America. He became professor of Scandinavian languages and literature at the University of Wisconsin in 1875, the first such chair at any American university. For many years he was editor of *Amerika*. (See *post*, n. 8.) While Anderson was gathering material for his volume on immigration he got in touch with Mrs. Wærenskjold.

with the book: it did not contain any history of Norway, as the advertisement promised.[5]

But please forgive an old woman for her ramblings, which perhaps bore you.

With the greatest respect,
ELISE WÆRENSKJOLD

The Norwegian Settlements

PRAIRIEVILLE
KAUFMAN COUNTY, TEXAS
July 3, 1894

MOST HONORED PROFESSOR [*R. B. Anderson*]:

It was a great pleasure to receive your friendly letter, for which I heartily thank you, as well as for the rest of the material you sent me. I have read most of it with much interest. As I read about your parents in *Billed-magazin*, it amused me to think how much greater a man you are than your mother's proud relatives! That class pride in Norway is indeed insufferable; but I hope that in this respect matters have improved since I left there in 1847.

I, too, am much interested in the history of the Norwegian settlements, but if it is merely published in *Amerika* and is not later organized and revised in book form, it will soon be lost, since most people destroy their newspapers when they have been read. I wrote an account of the first settlements in Texas for *Billed-magazin*; but I suppose few people have kept their copies. This magazine had many subscribers in Four Mile Prairie, but I am the only one who saved it. Many valuable sketches about the first immigrants to America are to be found there. As you will see by the enclosed letter, I have en-

---

[5] *De hjem vi forlod og de hjem vi fandt* (The Homes We Left and the Homes We Found — Chicago, Eau Claire, Wisconsin, 1892, 1893) was published anonymously. The preface stated that the book's purpose was to maintain among the ever-increasing Scandinavian population of this country a love for the homes they had left and to give them a clear conception of the great land to which they had come. The first 224 pages deal with Norway and, to some extent, with Sweden; the rest are about the United States.

deavored to persuade the first Norwegian [who settled] in Bosque [*Ole Canuteson*] to fulfill his promise to write an account of that settlement. I have been thinking of paying him a visit next month, and I shall then see if we cannot get a brief history written of the Norwegian settlements in Texas.

A Professor [John J.] Anderson, who lived in Austin, Texas, for several years, received $25 to write a biography of Cleng Peerson, which was to be included in a book about the first settlers here. But the book was never written, and consequently the biography was printed only in an American weekly. I suppose some of the Norwegians in Bosque were sufficiently interested to save it, and when I get there this fall, I shall make it my business to secure a copy.[6]

It seems to me that Johan Reinert Reiersen as well as old Cleng Peerson deserves special mention because of his influence on immigration. He was the one who really brought Norwegians to Texas. So I wrote his oldest son [Oscar], who is cashier in a bank in Key West, Florida, and received in return an account of the family's journey from Norway to Texas.

I would like very much to read O. N. Nelson's book, but unfortunately it is much too expensive for me. Presumably it would be better to include an account of the Texas settlements in his book (a supplement is to come) than in *Amerika*. I have written him to inquire if he would like a biography of Reiersen and an article about Texas. I cannot write it in English, but I suppose it could be translated. I write letters in English, but it is another matter with things that are to be published.[7]

In conclusion, a few words about who I am. My mother and father were Danes. Father was a pastor, first at Dybvaag, where I was born, later at West Moland, and, last, at Holt, where he died in 1832. For over three years I was married to Svend Foyn, but due to incompatibility — absolutely nothing else — we agreed to a friendly separation, and he has truly proved to be a friend by sending me money several times after my second husband was murdered by a scoundrel of a Methodist preacher [N. T. Dickerson] in 1866. I have two sons;

[6] On Professor John J. Anderson, see *ante*, part 3, n. 14.
[7] Olof Nicholaus Nelson, ed., *History of the Scandinavians and Successful Scandinavians in the United States* (Minneapolis, 1893–97). This work is devoted largely to immigration from the northern countries and to Scandinavian church bodies and educational institutions in the United States.

the older lives in Hamilton County, where I visit him every autumn. While there I also spend some time with our countrymen in Bosque, many of whom formerly lived here.

Pardon, dear professor, if I have tired you with my long letter.

With sincerest respect,

Yours truly,

ELISE WÆRENSKJOLD

Reiersen Must Not Be Overlooked[8]

[PRAIRIEVILLE, August 25, 1894?]

[TO THE EDITOR:]

If the men who contributed substantially to emigration deserve a special place in the history of our settlements, then Johan Reinert Reiersen must not be overlooked. He exerted influence both by means of his paper, *Christianssandsposten*, and by taking a trip through several states to discover where conditions would be most suitable for Norwegians to locate. Furthermore, after his return from this trip, he published a book about America, and, prior to his final departure, undertook the publication of a fly sheet, *Norge og Amerika*, which ran for three years — and it is due to him alone that Norwegian settlements were founded in Texas.

Johan Reinert Reiersen was born April 17, 1810, in the sexton's cabin at West Moland. His father, Ole Reiersen, was sexton there but later moved to Holt. Ole Reiersen had seven sons and two daughters; Johan Reinert was the oldest. As the boy seemed to be unusually gifted, the father determined to let him study at the university. But since this was no easy matter, considering the small salary that a country sexton received, the son was a tutor for awhile at the home of a Mr. Holm in Tvedestrand. Because of a youthful indiscretion, he

---

[8] This letter appeared in *Amerika*, September 12, 1894. *Amerika* was a weekly published in Chicago, 1885–97, later in Madison, Wisconsin, until its demise in 1922. Its editors (Thrond Bothne, O. M. Kalheim, Peer Strømme, R. B. Anderson) were well known among the Norwegian Americans of the Middle West; it engaged in many heated political and religious controversies with other Norwegian-American periodicals. Luther College at Decorah has a file of *Amerika*.

was forced to leave the University of Christiania; he went to Copenhagen, where, for several years, he supported himself by translating German and French books in collaboration with E. F. Gyntelberg.[9]

In Copenhagen he married his first wife, Henriette Waldt, by whom he had five sons and two daughters. (She died at Prairieville early in 1851 following the premature birth of her youngest son.) From Copenhagen he went to Hamburg. After a brief stay there, he returned to Norway and in Christiansand began publishing *Christianssandsposten*. Through it he worked for public enlightenment, freedom of conscience, Christian tolerance, the development of public spirit, and the freedom and independence of the nation. Furthermore, he did everything in his power to check the liquor evil, and because of this some people who wished to ridicule him called him "the apostle of temperance." He succeeded in setting up the first temperance society in the cathedral city, after which he organized similar societies in neighboring parishes, and then more and more in ever-widening circles. Frequently Reiersen criticized the shortcomings of officials, and he was always ready to side with the poor against the abuses by those in power. It is easy to understand that in this way he created not a few enemies. The fact that his paper gave much information about America and encouraged emigration greatly displeased many, for such activity was then considered almost treasonable.

Among Reiersen's bitterest enemies was Adolf Stabell, the editor of *Morgenbladet*, yet I myself have heard Stabell say that Reiersen was the ablest editor in Norway. When it was learned that Reiersen wanted to emigrate, one of his friends, Christian Grøgaard, son of the *Eidsvoldsmand*, Pastor Hans Jacob Grøgaard, proposed that we induce him to go alone first and investigate which places in America were most suitable for Norwegian settlers. For this undertaking we agreed to guarantee him 300 *spesiedaler*. Reiersen accepted the offer, although the amount did not fully cover his expenses and he had

---

[9] Ole Reiersen's daughter Gina married Andreas Ørbeck, and, after his death, a Swede named Hallin. Ole's son Christian had married Ouline Ørbeck before they left Norway; after he died she became the wife of J. R. Reiersen. Gerhard settled in Nacogdoches. Carl and Lassen moved to Wisconsin, but later returned to Texas, and Andreas moved to Chicago. Lina married Mads Vinzent and they went to California. Johan Reinert died in 1864. This information has been gleaned from Mrs. Wærenskjold's letters, but a granddaughter of Carl states that he moved, not to Wisconsin, but to Buffalo, New York. Virginia Carl Woods to Mrs. L. M. George, April 16, 1961. Georg Reiersen went into the commission business in Shreveport.

to give his time free — no small sacrifice for a family man without means.[10]

In the summer of 1843 he left Norway for New Orleans by way of Havre de Grace in France, thence to the Northern states. After he had visited the various Norwegian settlements then in existence, he wrote a brief account of his observations and sent it to Norway. The reliability of this account was vouched for by Hans Gasmann, Pastor Unonius, and others. Later he [*Reiersen*] also went to Texas, then an independent republic. From a travel letter written in Cincinnati on March 19, 1844, we notice that he went by stage from Natchitoches, Louisiana, to San Augustine, Texas, then to Austin, the capital [of Texas]. Their congress was in session at the time, and Reiersen readily secured an audience with the governor [*president*], General Sam Houston, who expressed great interest in having Norwegian emigrants choose Texas as their new fatherland.

After five days in Austin he went through the towns of Bastrop and Rutersville to Washington on the Brazos River, thence to Houston and Galveston, where he arrived March 7. From there he went by steamboat to New Orleans. After his return to Norway, he published a rather large book, *Veiviser for norske emigranter*. Each of the group who had guaranteed the 300 *spesiedaler* received a free copy. Before he left again, he and his brother Christian together began the publication of *Norge og Amerika*. Through these works he contributed not a little to the cause of emigration.

In April, 1845, Reiersen, accompanied by Christian Grøgaard and Syvert Nielsen, went by ship from Lillesand to Havre de Grace, where they met Reiersen's father [Ole], his oldest sister Lina, and his brother Gerhard, who had come from Arendal on another ship. As the vessels were already filled, the whole party could not find quarters on the same vessel. From Havre they went to New Orleans on an American ship. There Sexton [Ole] Reiersen bought a land certificate for 1,446 acres in Texas, and from the Texas consul in New Orleans

[10] Adolf Bredo Stabell (1807–65) was an influential Norwegian politician, financier, and journalist. In 1831 he became editor of *Morgenbladet*, then a rather insignificant newspaper. Under his shrewd, energetic leadership it became the principal organ of the parliamentary opposition to the royal cabinet and the official bureaucracy. In 1857 Stabell was succeeded by Christian Friele, under whose direction the paper became staunchly conservative. The title *Eidsvoldsmand* identifies Hans J. Grøgaard as one of the framers of the Norwegian constitution of 1814.

they obtained a letter of introduction to Dr. [James H.] Starr in Nacogdoches.[11]

From New Orleans they went by boat up the Mississippi and Red rivers to Natchitoches, Louisiana; from there Gerhard Reiersen, Grøgaard, and Nielsen continued on to Shreveport and Marshall; J. R. Reiersen, his father, and Lina went overland to Nacogdoches, where they arrived on the Fourth of July. There was a ball in honor of the occasion to which they were invited, and they were shown much hospitality. In Nacogdoches [J. R.] Reiersen got in touch with a German merchant named Hoya and a man from Schleswig by the name of G. Bondiz, also a merchant. These men showed much good will to Reiersen, as they did to later Norwegian immigrants. Hoya took Reiersen to Dr. Starr, who went to the land office with him to check the validity of the certificate his father had bought. He also promised that he would introduce him to a surveyor who could be trusted.

Toward fall they set out to look for land and decided to locate where the Brownsboro community is now. This was the beginning of the first Norwegian settlement in Texas, and they called it Normandy. Reiersen, after helping his father buy the necessary animals and hiring an American to build a log house for his family, set off for New Orleans to meet his wife and children, his mother, and his sister Gina. I will let his son Oscar, who is now a cashier at a bank in Key West, Florida, tell about the family's trip from Norway to Texas :[12]

"My mother with my self, John, Carl, Christian and infant daughter, Henriette, took sailing vessel from Kristianssand in late summer or fall, proceeding to Havre de Grace, France, with grandmother and Gina. At Havre we remained some 10 days and then boarded the sailing ship *Magnolia*, with a number of other Norwegian families, bound for New Orleans, La. On the route little Henriette died and was consigned to the waves.

"We took lodgings in New Orleans, remaining there several

---

[11] In earlier letters, Mrs. Wærenskjold gave the amount of land as 1,476 acres; see *ante*, p. 78, 80. On Starr, see *ante*, part 2, n. 22.

[12] Oscar Reiersen's account, written in English, was interpolated in that form in Mrs. Wærenskjold's letter. It is here given precisely as it appeared in *Amerika*, without correction or editing. The boy Carl who appears in this narrative was presumably J. R. Reiersen's son, rather than his brother. The latter grew up to raise a family. See *ante*, n. 9. The "Gin House" in which the Reiersens first lodged in Texas was apparently the building that housed a cotton gin.

months. The Grøgaards were there. After a time uncle Lassen came there from Chicago, and later father. We proceeded for Shreveport up Red River on a very small steamboat. Water was very low, and no passage over the falls at Alexandria. A week was spent before they succeeded in winding our little boat over the falls by hawsers fastened to trees up the river bank and capstan worked on boat. Slowly we went up the river. Seven miles above Natchitoches a little after dark, the boat run on a snag. We all got in a canebracke. Boat was lost, wet provisions being fished out of the boats cargo, diving for which, to attack rope or hook to barrels or bales, father was nearly drowned, being hauled up unconscious after having gone down successfully several times. No chance to get away till rain above should swell the river, so that boats could ascend. This was two weeks, during which muddy river water was our only drink and we were exposed to rains etc. All our movable effects, except some light boxes or trunks, were lost in this wreck. At Shreveport, being with but slender means, we lived in a cabin, we boys all down with diarrhoe and I with measles in addition. For weeks I was not able to turn in bed, a Dr. Black in attendance. I was delirious often. One evening Black with other physicians examined me with father and mother at the bedside. They decided I could not last through the night — that I was dying then, extremities growing cold. This was in 1846 in the winter. Now it is 1894. I am not dead yet and have had but little faith in the medical art since. They left. Father heated bricks and rocks which rolled in carpets and blankets were piled round me, which doubtless saved me. It is as distinct in memory as if it had occurred but yesterday. Later we moved to a better house on the Bayou above the town, where boarders were taken for a time. Here Carl died. It was spring when Carl and I some few days before were out plucking some flowers and my wrist was dislocated by rail falling on it. Some time after we were hauled in a wagon with our little plunder into Texas, some three miles from the later town of Mount Enterprise in Rusk Co. Charles Vincent had a little country store and we lived in a Gin House. Father had met Vincent in Shreveport and been helped by him. We children were fearfully weak, but recuperated at that Gin, where we got an abundance of buttermilk. We were there some time before we were hauled up to father's house in Brownsboro Settlement

1846. Grandmother and Gina with Lassen left us when we got to Shreveport."

Several Norwegian families and one that was Danish came at Christmastime, 1846, and settled near Reiersen's place, but, directly contrary to his advice, about eight families crowded together in a little house on bottom land that they rented from an American who would not live in it because of its unhealthful location. During the summer of 1847 all of these people took sick; several died and undoubtedly still more would have if Reiersen had not gone to Cherokee County for medicine, and then tended them without charging anything except for the medicine.

At New Year's, 1848, he and his family moved to Four Mile Prairie, where he later founded the little town of Prairieville. Several years after the death of his first wife [*1851*] he married his brother Christian's widow, Ouline Jacobine Ørbeck, daughter of Ørbeck, the Lillesand merchant. This marriage was childless, but of the children from his first marriage the following are still living: Oscar; John, who has a large hotel in Kaufman; and Christian, who lives in the Indian Territory. The two first mentioned are married to American women. Reiersen died September 6, 1864, in Prairieville, where his widow still lives.

[ELISE WÆRENSKJOLD]

Everyone Was So Friendly

PRAIRIEVILLE
November 14, 1894

MY DEAR MARIE:

At last I am home again after traveling a little more than three months. I really had an enjoyable trip, because everyone was so friendly and kind to me. I am now beginning to sell out, but it goes very slowly; there is little money here, because people get practically nothing for their cotton. Many behaved so foolishly as to hold the crop in the hope that prices would rise. Thus Eastvold and Nils

Gilbert, both really good farmers, have not sold a single bale. The crop was good, if only they could get something for it. Two babies came to Knudsen's family in one year while I was away, and Julie Small was so sick that they thought she would die, but now she is well. Lena Annonsen has also been very sick. I did not get home until last Thursday, so I haven't yet seen many of my neighbors.[13]

(Later the same day.) Tulla Knudsen interrupted me, and later Betha Wattner and Mrs. Mjaaland. All of them are well. Niels is poorly but works all the time. The children pick cotton, except the oldest and the youngest ones.

It was so very pleasant at Beruld Olsen's in Dallas, because Helene Persen and Anne Olsen were there at the same time. We went to the fair together and to Berthea Eastvold's. She has a new little son. They have bought three acres of land, on which there is a little house, for $11. Tomorrow Elef Albertsen's daughter, who is a music teacher, will celebrate her wedding. I feel that they ought to wait until Monday the nineteenth, because then it will be twenty-six years since her parents were married — and both of them still look so young. Knud Mjaaland moved into his new house yesterday. Wattner built it for him.

I borrowed the church register, but unfortunately it does not give the date of his [*your father's*] death. It merely states that he was born in Lauenburg March 1, 1815, and that he came to Texas in 1846 and died — nothing more, not even the year of his death.[14]

I met Anton Aanonsen last Sunday, and he said that he and his wife are in good health now. In four weeks I hope to be ready to leave. I will go through Bosque, as I usually do, since it is very difficult for one as old as I am to go to a strange place. Olsen has promised to meet me at the station when I arrive in Dallas, and the next day he will help me get on the other train. The Andersens promised me that when I arrive in Clifton they will take me to Hansen's; and if Otto is not altogether too busy he can meet me

[13] According to tradition, Mrs. Wærenskjold was a sort of walking newspaper and went on foot from settlement to settlement when her friends and neighbors were not able to provide her with transportation. She was welcomed "just like a bishop"; the special foods that she preferred were prepared for her; Mrs. Henry J. Gould to the editor, April 7, 1961. Mrs. Wærenskjold was "selling out" in 1894 because she was preparing to live with Otto in Hamilton. The new babies were Knudsen's grandchildren.

[14] Marie Jensen's father was J. H. Staack.

there. My goods, however, I will send from Wills Point to Cisco and from there to Hico.

I suppose you know that Olsen, the schoolteacher, accompanied the minister [*Rystad*] to Four Mile. Kirsti Olsen has bought a good organ. They took it to the church and Olsen played on it. I am so curious to hear what he thought of our settlement. A Norwegian family from Dallas is moving here. The man, Gundersen, works at the cotton gin, but the family cannot come until Oscar builds a house for them.

Well, now I do not know any more to write about, so I will end with a sincere greeting to all of you.

Your devoted

ELISE WÆRENSKJOLD

Probably the Last Trip

PRAIRIEVILLE

November 15, 1894

To MRS. THOMINE DANNEVIG:

A week ago I returned from my trip — I had been away for three months. A long stay, but it is probably the last trip I shall make, for I have decided to move to my son Otto's and to settle down peacefully with him for the rest of my days. My health is still good, but I am not nearly so strong as I used to be and it is quite difficult for me to carry on my work in the house and garden, as I have done up to now. I am going to have a room to myself at Otto's and take my meals with the family. Life will be easier for me; but it will be very hard to leave my dear old home where I have now lived for forty-six years. It is sad to think that I may never again see Niels and the dear children or my other relatives, and my kind old neighbors, for I shall be too old to take trips alone. As you know, I shall be eighty in February.

I had a very pleasant trip. First I spent two days with Mother Pabst and then a week in Tyler at the home of a niece [*Fanny Skjolden*] of my husband. At the same time I visited the other two Norwegian families who live there. One is a merchant by the name of [Elef] Albertsen; his wife's parents [*Jens and Berte Halvorsen*] were the poorest Norwegian couple ever to come to Texas, but honest and industrious. Now all of their six daughters have married well and the son married a daughter of Governor Roberts. From Tyler I went to Waco to the home of one of the most prominent Norwegians in Texas, where I remained almost a week and visited Mother's relatives and a few other Norwegians whom I knew. Ole Canuteson, my host, was the first Norwegian to settle in Bosque, where there are now about two thousand Scandinavians, and two Norwegian churches. I spent three weeks at Otto's and six weeks in Bosque.[15]

Otto is still only a constable, and his earnings are rather small. He is well liked; but there are three political parties here and people feel bound to vote for a member of their own party. He is a Democrat, and many of his friends belong to the Populist party. Ophelia, his wife, earns a little by weaving rugs for people. They have a good house with six rooms, and so much land that they have quite a few fruit trees and room for more garden products and potatoes, both Norwegian and sweet varieties, than they need for their own use.

The last places I visited were Dallas and Kaufman, and I had a pleasant time everywhere, for all were friendly and kind to me. Knudsen [Ole Canuteson], in Waco, wanted me to visit him [again] on the way home and even offered to pay my fare from Waco to Dallas; but I didn't have time to be away any longer, because I leave for Otto's four weeks from now and I have several things to sell.

We have had a delightful but very dry autumn, so it has been fine for the many cotton pickers. There is a great deal of cotton this year, but unfortunately the price is lower than it has ever been. Though the price was more than $.06 a pound at the beginning, many people were so foolish as to wait for a better market, and now it has gone down to $.04. So things are bad for the farmers in spite of the good crop, especially for those who have to hire pickers. Of Niels's seven children, all except the oldest and the youngest pick cotton.

If you are in Tønsberg, you must show this letter to Lovise Seeberg. I know she has not forgotten her old teacher and will no doubt cheer me with a letter soon.

[15] Oran Milo Roberts (1815–98), a prominent Texas jurist and politician, was elected governor in 1878 and 1880. His daughter, Fannie U. Roberts, married S. Christian Halvorsen, a brother of Mrs. Elef Albertsen. Information furnished by Derwood Johnson and by the Texas State Historical Association at Austin. On Ole Canuteson, see *ante*, part 2, n. 29.

To you and all your family, and to my dear Lovise, I wish a very happy Christmas and a good and blessed New Year.

With affectionate greetings to you all,

> Your
> [E. WÆRENSKJOLD]

Until God Calls Me

> HAMILTON
> HAMILTON COUNTY, TEXAS
> December 26, 1894

MOST HONORED PROFESSOR [R. B. Anderson]:

I noted in *Norden* that you are going to write about the first Norse settlements in the United States and that among other sources you plan to use Elling Eielsen's biography. As it contains several inaccuracies about church conditions in Texas during the first years, I shall take the liberty of giving you a correct account.[16]

The first Norwegian settlement was established by the editor of *Christianssandsposten*, Johan Reinert Reiersen, in 1845. Reiersen and a few others, among them Christian Grøgaard from Lillesand, left in the spring and came to Texas in early July, 1845. A larger party was to follow in the fall of the year. At that time they had already considered securing a Norwegian schoolteacher and minister, namely Christian Grøgaard, son of the *Eidsvoldsmand* and textbook author, H[ans] J. Grøgaard. In his youth he (Christian Grøgaard) had studied theology.

This party had chartered two vessels to take them to Havre de Grace. Unfortunately the leaders quarreled with the owner of one of the ships, who really was an unreasonable and perverse individual. Thus, half the group had to wait until the next year, as no other vessel was available that fall; they never got to Texas. Most of those who arrived on the latter ship were from Setesdal, and when they got to New Orleans they let themselves be scared out of going to Texas. They went up the Mississippi, which, at that time of the year, was full of ice; so they suffered a great deal before they reached their destina-

---

[16] This account of Eielsen's life is identified *ante*, part 1, n. 13.

tion. Only the Reiersens, the Grøgaards, and one other family came
to Texas. The next year, however, at Christmastime, a party of immigrants came to the newly established settlement, and, in the summer
of 1847, I too came to Texas. For a time I stayed with Grøgaard's
widow at Nacogdoches. Grøgaard and the two youngest children had
died.

Early in October I went to the settlement, then called Normandy,
that was later renamed Brownsboro. About fifteen families were there
at that time; unfortunately, most of them were sick and dissatisfied,
and several had died. The main reason for this, undoubtedly, was that
they had crowded together on low, unhealthful locations, while the
Reiersens, who had built a rather large house on somewhat higher
ground, were in good health.

Afterwards more and more immigrants came; in 1847 a new settlement was begun at Four Mile Prairie, where I purchased land. In
the fall of that year, I married Wilhelm Wærenskjold; I lived there
for forty-six years, but now I have moved away to live with my oldest
son [Otto] in Hamilton.

Dean [Jakob F.] Fridrichsen was my father's successor at West
Moland, and I often received letters from his wife. She wrote me early
in 1853 that her son, Anders Emil Fridrichsen, a theological candidate,
wished to come to us as our pastor. This offer was accepted by the
Norwegians in Brownsboro and Four Mile Prairie. The first Norwegian Lutheran church in Texas was built at Four Mile Prairie
the following winter. Pastor Fridrichsen served these two congregations for three years and also made several trips to Bosque County,
where a new settlement had been founded.

Before we had our first pastor, and after he left, we ourselves
ministered as best we could at baptisms and funerals. My husband, or
perhaps someone who had been a schoolteacher in Norway, baptized
the children according to the Norwegian ritual. (I had brought my
father's altar book with me.) They performed the ceremony of scat-
tering earth upon the casket and delivering the funeral orations. We
also had Sunday school, and my husband organized a temperance
society at Four Mile. Intoxicating liquor was absolutely forbidden
at our gatherings, and the men did not get drunk when they went to
town.

We were especially pleased with Elling Eielsen's visit, and I wish that all our pastors were as zealous for a practical, working Christianity as he was. Then there would not be so much drinking among the Norwegians as now. Our temperance society died when the Synod pastors told us that it was a sin for us to join such an organization — something that they certainly can never make me believe.

I see that I have been more loquacious than I had intended, and I hope you will forgive me. I cannot believe that Elling Eielsen has himself presented the situation in Texas as that book describes it. We were no more godless then, nor did we lead more unchristian lives at that time than we do now when we have three pastors.

I arrived in Hamilton last week, and it is my intention to remain here until God calls me away.

With true respect,
Elise Wærenskjold

An Interest in History [17]

Hamilton
January 10, 1894 [<i>1895</i>]</div>

Honored Professor:

Your valued letter was received last week. As I was certain that Ole Canuteson (in whose home Cleng Peerson lived several years, and who was a neighbor of [Johannes] Nordboe in Dallas) could give a better account than I of these men, I sent your letter to him, requesting that he return it with his notations. Yesterday I was informed that he had heard from you and had sent a reply.

To the best of my knowledge, Nordboe was the first Norwegian to settle in Texas, but I do not know when he came. He was living in Dallas County when we arrived, and I believe he had been there all the time. I think he came from the north coast of Norway. Had I known that this matter would arouse such great interest, I could certainly have induced him to write his autobiography. He liked to write and read, and even spent time drawing and carving in stone. He

---

[17] In this letter to R. B. Anderson, Mrs. Wærenskjold mistakenly wrote the date 1894 instead of 1895. Toward the close she mentions the death of Svend Foyn, which did not occur until late in 1894.

was a small, very frail-looking man of about eighty. He held his countrymen in warm regard, and when he heard about the Reiersens and Wærenskjolds, nothing could hold him back; he insisted on visiting us. He could not endure riding horseback, and his sons, who did not share their father's interests, would not bring him over, so the old man set out on foot the long way from Dallas to Four Mile Prairie and arrived shortly before Christmas, in 1851. After the holidays, Cleng Peerson came to accompany him home, but I do not think Nordboe was very happy about it, as it was too strenuous for him to keep up with Cleng. Nordboe seemed to be a very kind man, and he took a great interest in the study of history and the wonders of nature.

I have not heard any mention of the Johnsen who is supposed to have arrived in Texas in 1829. We did find a Dane here, Nicolai Hansen, from Elsinore, who lived in Texas many years, having come here as a seaman. He became ill and was nursed by an American widow, whom he later married; thus he stayed in the country. But he had no influence on the immigration movement, which likely would not have struck Texas for many years had not Reiersen directed attention to this state.

Both of the first settlements that Reiersen established were in Henderson County. Buffalo, on the Trinity River, a little town long since abandoned, was the county seat. Henderson County was divided, but Brownsboro, the oldest settlement, is still in Henderson County. Four Mile Prairie was divided, too, so that half of the settlement lies in Van Zandt County and the other half in Kaufman County. My home was in Van Zandt; [J. R.] Reiersen's was in Kaufman County.

It is impossible for me to recall when Cleng Peerson first came to Texas, but I do know for certain that it was not before 1849. Therefore he did not come with Nordboe. When Cleng came the second time, the [Ole] Canuteson family was with him; otherwise he had little influence on immigration to this state. I know nothing about the immigration of the years 1838 and 1839. My mother died in 1839; that same year I married Svend Foyn and had not the slightest interest in emigration.

Most of the Norwegians in Texas are from Hedmark. The first two who came from there on the advice of Andreas Gjestvang, postmaster in Løiten, Hedmark, were an old schoolteacher, Engelhoug, and an elderly farmer, Knud Olsen. This man was a capable worker and an upright person. His daughter and her children live in good circumstances in Bosque.

Gjestvang subscribed to the paper [*Norge og Amerika*] that [Johan] Reinert and Christian Reiersen published. When the latter also went to America in 1846, no one wanted to put out such a dangerous sheet, that might lure people into migrating. To keep the paper alive, I undertook its publication. One fine day Gjestvang came to Christiania to interview the publisher and was not a little surprised to find that E. Tvede was a woman. After that, I often had letters from him.

As people then listened eagerly for everything uncomplimentary to America, *Hamars budstikke* made an exceptional haul when it got hold of a French "romance," or kind of travelogue, about Texas. Gjestvang took the trouble to copy the whole strange work and sent it to me with a request to comment on it. This I did, and many Norwegians, among them Nordboe and Cleng Peerson, added their impressions. A little later my husband wrote an article on the same subject, which I am sending you in case it may possibly interest you. All this was published in *Hamars budstikke* and later appeared in pamphlet form. This contributed not a little to the emigration to Texas. All the newcomers came directly to our house and stopped several days, or weeks, with us — one family even stayed six months. I regret that I cannot answer your questions any better.

Yes, Svend Foyn is dead. I received the account of his grand funeral from a friend in Tønsberg. The widow is said to retain undivided possession of the estate; but after her death, the greater part of the large fortune goes to the mission. Neither his native land nor his birthplace gets anything.[18]

With high esteem,
Yours respectfully,
ELISE WÆRENSKJOLD

Has *Amerika* done anything with Ole Canuteson's biography?

[18] This statement about Foyn's will is somewhat misleading. He provided that after the death of his second wife, the major portion of his fortune be set aside to help support foreign missions and schools for missionaries. Certain sums, however, were earmarked for aid to various charitable and religious institutions in Norway. See Johan Austbø, *Svend Foyn: Mannen og verket hans*, 73 (Oslo, 1942).

Index

Index

For the convenience of readers the Norwegian characters æ and ø are alphabeted as *ae* and *o*, respectively.

173

SCANDINAVIANS IN AMERICA

An Arno Press Collection

Ander, O. Fritiof. **The Cultural Heritage of the Swedish Immigrant:** Selected References. [1956]

Ander, Oscar Fritiof. **T.N. Hasselquist:** The Career and Influence of a Swedish American Clergyman, Journalist and Editor. 1931

Barton, H. Arnold, editor. **Clipper Ship and Covered Wagon:** Essays From the *Swedish Pioneer Historical Quarterly.* 1979

Blegen, Theodore C. and Martin B. Ruud, editors and translators. **Norwegian Emigrant Songs and Ballads.** Songs harmonized by Gunnar J. Maimin. 1936

Christensen, Thomas Peter. **A History of the Danes in Iowa.** 1952

Duus, Olaus Fredrik. **Frontier Parsonage:** The Letters of Olaus Fredrik Duus, Norwegian Pastor in Wisconsin, 1855-1858. Translated by the Verdandi Study Club of Minneapolis. Edited by Theodore C. Blegen. 1947

Erickson, E. Walfred. **Swedish-American Periodicals:** A Selective Bibliography. 1979

Gjerset, Knut. **Norwegian Sailors in American Waters:** A Study in the History of Maritime Activity on the Eastern Seaboard. 1933

Gjerset, Knut. **Norwegian Sailors on the Great Lakes:** A Study in the History of American Inland Transportation. 1928

Hale, Frederick. **Trans-Atlantic Conservative Protestantism in the Evangelical Free and Mission Covenant Traditions** (Doctoral Thesis, The Johns Hopkins University, 1976, Revised Edition). 1979

Hogland, A. William. **Finnish Immigrants in America:** 1880-1920. 1960

Hokanson, Nels. **Swedish Immigrants in Lincoln's Time.** With a Foreword by Carl Sandberg. 1942

Hummasti, Paul George. **Finnish Radicals in Astoria, Oregon, 1904-1940:** A Study in Immigrant Socialism (Doctoral Dissertation, University of Oregon, 1975, Revised Edition). 1979

Hustvedt, Lloyd. **Rasmus Bjørn Anderson:** Pioneer Scholar. 1966

Jenson, Andrew. **History of the Scandinavian Mission.** 1927

Kolehmainen, John I. **Sow the Golden Seed:** A History of the Fitchburg (Massachusetts) Finnish American Newspaper, Raivaaja, (The Pioneer), 1905-1955. 1955

Kolehmainen, John I. and George W. Hill. **Haven in the Woods:** The Story of the Finns in Wisconsin. 1965

Koren, Elisabeth. **The Diary of Elisabeth Koren:** 1853-1855. Translated and Edited by David T. Nelson. 1955

Larson, Esther Elisabeth. **Swedish Commentators on America, 1638-1865:** An Annotated List of Selected Manuscript and Printed Materials. 1963

Lindeström, Peter. **Geographia Americae With An Account of the Delaware Indians.** 1925

Marzolf, Marion Tuttle. **The Danish Language Press in America** (Doctoral Dissertation, the University of Michigan, 1972). 1979

McKnight, Roger. **Moberg's Emigrant Novels and the *Journals* of Andrew Peterson:** A Study of Influences and Parallels (Doctoral Thesis, the University of Minnesota, 1974). 1979

Mattson, Hans. **Reminiscences:** The Story of an Immigrant. 1891

Mortenson, Enok. **Danish-American Life and Letters:** A Bibliography. 1945

Nelson, Helge. **The Swedes and the Swedish Settlements in North America.** 1943. 2 vols. in 1

Nielson, Alfred C. **Life in an American Denmark.** 1962

Olson, Ernst W., Anders Schon and Martin J. Engberg, editors. **History of the Swedes of Illinois.** 1908. 2 vols.

Puotinen, Arthur Edwin. **Finnish Radicals and Religion in Midwestern Mining Towns,** 1865-1914 (Doctoral Dissertation, the University of Chicago, 1973). 1979

Raaen, Aagot. **Grass of the Earth:** Immigrant Life in the Dakota Country. 1950

Scott, Franklin D. **Trans-Atlantica:** Essays on Scandinavian Migration and Culture. 1979

Strombeck, Rita. **Leonard Strömberg—A Swedish-American Writer** (Doctoral Thesis, the University of Chicago, 1975, Revised Edition). 1979

Svendsen, Gro. **Frontier Mother:** The Letters of Gro Svendsen. Translated and edited by Pauline Farseth and Theodore C. Blegen. 1950

Vogel-Jorgensen, T[homas]. **Peter Lassen Af California.** 1937

Waerenskjold, Elise. **The Lady with the Pen:** Elise Waerenskjold in Texas. Edited by C.A. Clausen with a foreword by Theodore C. Blegen. 1961

Weintraub, Hyman. **Andrew Furuseth:** Emancipator of the Seamen. 1959

Winther, Sophus Keith. **Mortgage Your Heart.** 1937